**St Michael**

# Here's Health

# SEASONAL
# VEGETARIAN

*St Michael*

**Here's Health**

# SEASONAL VEGETARIAN

*Sarah Bounds*

## Note

**1** All recipes serve four unless otherwise stated.
**2** All spoon measurements are level.
**3** All eggs are sizes 3, 4 unless otherwise stated. Although free-range eggs are specified throughout, you can use ordinary eggs when the former are unobtainable.
**4** Preparation times given are an average calculated during recipe testing.
**5** Metric and Imperial measurements have been calculated separately. Use one set of measurements only as they are not exact equivalents.
**6** Cooking times may vary slightly depending on the individual oven. Dishes should be placed in the centre of the oven unless otherwise specified.
**7** Always preheat the oven or grill to the specified temperature.
**8** Although these recipes do not contain salt, you can add a little to taste, if preferred.

Front cover, central photograph, from the top, *Winter salad bowl (page 76); Strawberry choux puffs (page 42); Spinach-stuffed pancakes (page 18); Lentil sauce (page 21).* Left-hand photograph, *Ratatouille (page 34).* Right-hand photograph, *Mange-tout and tofu stir-fry (page 35).* Back cover, *Chestnut pie (page 74); Cheesy baked potatoes (page 74).*

Published 1986 by The Hamlyn Publishing Group Ltd,
Bridge House, London Road,
Twickenham, Middlesex

Copyright © Argus Health Publications Limited 1986

Photography by David Jordan
Styling by Pip Kelly

ISBN 0 600 32667 5

Printed in Italy

# CONTENTS

# INTRODUCTION

Healthy eating from January to December is the aim of this book. With the emphasis firmly on vegetarian meals to suit the season, I hope that there is something for everyone to enjoy, including those not committed to vegetarian eating. As the recipes in each of the four sections show, a vegetarian diet is fun and full of variety whether it be the depths of winter or the height of summer.

### Planning a Healthy Diet without Meat

Most people's first thoughts on becoming vegetarian, or simply on cutting down the amount of meat, fish and poultry in their diets are concerned with health. Is it possible to stay healthy without meat? Where do vitamins and minerals come from and what about protein? What can I eat instead of just cheese, eggs and milk? The answers to these questions are positive; cutting meat, fish and poultry from your diet does not mean that you will go short of vital nutrients like protein, vitamins and minerals. In fact, research suggests that a vegetarian diet is positively healthier than a non-vegetarian diet and that common problems like obesity are less likely to occur for vegetarians than their meat-eating neighbours.

### Protein Power

We all associate animal foods like meat, fish, eggs, cheese and milk with protein and it is true that these foods do all supply good levels of high-quality protein. Taken individually, foods of vegetable origin tend to be less concentrated sources of protein and the protein they do contain is of a lower quality.

However, provided a mixture of different kinds of vegetable food is eaten, the protein is of equally good quality to that in animal foods. The quality of protein in a food is assessed in terms of the amounts of the eight essential amino acids necessary for health, found in that food. Animal protein-containing foods contain all the essential amino acids and in amounts suitable to meet the body's needs; plant protein-containing foods on the other hand may lack one or more of the essential amino acids or contain an insufficient quantity.

Plant protein-containing foods fall into two main groups and each group is short of a different amino acid. To obtain the balance of the amino acids essential for the body at one time it is important to mix different plant foods together at one meal. So a pulse should be eaten with a grain or nut or seed and so on, as the chart below shows. Alternatively the shortage of amino acids in, say, rice, can be overcome by adding a dairy food—milk, egg or cheese—at the same meal.

Remembering the basic rule of combining plant protein foods will ensure that a vegetarian diet remains a healthy alternative to a diet which includes, or is based on, meat.

## COMBINING PLANT FOODS FOR PROTEIN

To make the most of the protein found in plant foods, combine pulses and grains or nuts or seeds at as many meals as possible.

### Pulses
*Beans:* butter, haricot, aduki, blackeye, flageolet, red and black kidney beans, pinto and soya beans.

*Lentils:* red, green and continental brown lentils.

*Peas:* green and yellow dried split peas.

### Grains, Nuts and Seeds
*Grains:* oats, wheat, barley, rye, millet, buckwheat, corn or maize, rice. These should be eaten preferably in the whole-grain state, or as flour milled from the whole grain.

*Nuts:* walnuts, hazelnuts, cashews, almonds, brazils, pecans, peanuts and chestnuts.

*Seeds:* sesame, sunflower and pumpkin.

## Fibre

Although individually animal foods may have a superior protein content to that of vegetable foods, they do not contain fibre. It is from plant foods that the dietary fibre so vital in a healthy diet, comes. Foods such as the protein-rich pulses, grains, nuts and seeds all supply fibre, as do fruits and vegetables. Ideally, foods should be eaten as little processed as possible to maximise fibre content – wholegrain cereals such as brown rice contain more fibre than their refined counterparts. Eating a vegetarian diet, with the emphasis on plant rather than animal foods, makes it far easier to include the 30 g recommended daily intake of fibre.

## Fat

Foods high in fat are concentrated sources of calories and are undesirable in a healthy diet. There is now universal agreement among doctors and nutritionists that the typical British diet contains far too much fat, and in particular that the amount of saturated fat should be reduced. We need to restrict fat intake to 115 g a day. Saturated fats tend to be found in animal foods such as meat, offal and dairy produce. Fish, poultry and plant foods are generally higher in polyunsaturated fatty acids which are desirable ingredients in the diet.

Eating a vegetarian diet tends to reduce the level of saturated fat in favour of polyunsaturated fat and this is seen as beneficial. However, avoid adding extra fat to food, which will undo some of the good achieved by eliminating meat from the diet. First, it is important to try to limit the amount of extra fat used in cooking – grilling, steaming and baking avoid the addition of extra fat, whereas roasting and frying usually involve adding quite large amounts of extra fat to food. Secondly, it is important not to swamp food in fat at the table – adding a knob of butter to cooked vegetables obviously boosts not just the amount of fat but the calories too. Thirdly, it's wise to watch out for highly processed foods which may contain much added fat that's 'hidden' – cakes, pastries and biscuits usually depend on a high level of fat for their flavour and texture, and should be restricted to treats.

The recipes in this book aim to help restrict the amount of fat being eaten and because they are vegetarian, they tend to contain the beneficial polyunsaturated fatty acids rather than the harmful saturated fats.

## Vitamins and Minerals

Eating a meat-free diet does not mean that the body is deprived of essential vitamins and minerals, any more than it is of protein or other important nutrients. Eating a wide range of different foods is the key to a healthy diet. This list should help you check that vital vitamins and minerals are present in your diet. The foods listed under each vitamin and mineral contain the vitamin or mineral in decreasing order of quantity, so the best sources are listed first. Try to ensure that each day your diet contains a good source of every nutrient.

## Vitamins

**A:** (plant foods contain carotene which the body converts to retinol, vitamin A). Carrots, parsley, spinach, turnip tops, spring greens, sweet potatoes, watercress, broccoli, melon, endives, pumpkin, apricots, lettuce, prunes, tomatoes, peaches, butter, margarine, cheese and eggs.

**B1 (thiamine):** brewer's yeast, yeast extract, brown rice, wheatgerm, nuts, soya flour, oats and wholemeal bread.

**B2 (riboflavin):** yeast extract, brewer's yeast, wheatgerm, cheese, eggs, wheatbran, soya flour, yogurt, milk, leafy green vegetables, pulses.

**B3 (niacin):** yeast extract, brewer's yeast, wheatbran, nuts, soya flour, wheat, cheese, dried fruit, wholemeal bread, brown rice, wheatgerm, oats, eggs, pulses.

**B6 (pyridoxine):** brewer's yeast, wheatbran, yeast extract, wheatgerm, oats, soya flour, bananas, whole wheat, nuts, brown rice, potatoes, leafy green vegetables, root vegetables, wholemeal bread and eggs.

**Pantothenic acid:** brewer's yeast, yeast extract, nuts, bran, wheatgerm, soya flour, eggs, oats, pulses, dried fruits, maize, rice and wholemeal bread.

**Biotin:** brewer's yeast, yeast extract, eggs, oats, wheatbran, wheatgerm, wholemeal bread, maize.

**Folic acid:** brewer's yeast, soya flour, wheatgerm, wheatbran, nuts, leafy green vegetables, pulses, oats, whole wheat, wholemeal bread, citrus fruits, bananas, cheese.

**B12 (cobalamin):** eggs, cheese, milk. Plant foods do not contain B12 so vegans need to take special care in obtaining this vitamin. Some fermented plant foods such as soya-based miso, do contain some B12, and manufacturers of yeast extract products sometimes add it to their product.

**C:** blackcurrants, guavas, parsley, kale, horseradish, broccoli tops, green peppers, tomato purée, Brussels sprouts, chives, lemons, cauliflower, watercress, strawberries, cabbage, oranges, mustard and cress, blackberries, gooseberries, grapefruit, lychees. Other fruit and vegetables contain less than 40 mg vitamin C in 100 g/4 oz.

**D:** eggs, goat's milk, cow's milk, butter and margarine, cheese. Vitamin D is also made in the body by the action of sunlight.

**E:** vegetable oils, nuts, muesli, eggs, brown rice, peas and beans.

## Minerals

There are many minerals known to be essential for health, some required in quite large amounts, others in comparatively small quantities. Some of these vital minerals are present in a wide range of foods and a shortage is unlikely to occur. Phosphorus, sodium and chlorine are three examples of abundant minerals. Sodium in particular is eaten in far greater quantities in Britain than is needed for health and there is some evidence to suggest that the excessive amounts of sodium often eaten are hazardous and perhaps likely to aggravate the problem of high blood pressure. Limiting the amount of sodium eaten as salt is not difficult and will not have harmful consequences (except for kidney patients whose diets need to be supervised in this respect). For this reason salt has been omitted from the recipes in this book, as it is widely added to processed foods such as cheese, bread, breakfast cereals and sodium itself is naturally present in many fresh fruits and vegetables.

These minerals apart, there are a number of minerals which the body needs in quite large quantities and these are listed here together with the foods containing the best quantities of each. Zinc is one mineral of particular significance to vegetarians and vegans because the zinc in plant foods is less well absorbed than that from animal foods, so it is important to eat zinc-rich food daily to ensure supply is adequate.

**Calcium:** hard cheeses, soft cheeses, nuts, pulses, milk, root vegetables, eggs, oatmeal, fruits, wholemeal flour, maize.
**Iron:** brewer's yeast, wheatbran, cocoa, soya flour, parsley, dried peaches, figs and apricots, oatmeal, spinach, wholemeal flour, prunes, wholemeal bread, beans, sultanas and raisins.
**Magnesium:** soya beans, nuts, brewer's yeast, wholemeal flour, brown rice, dried peas, wholemeal bread, rye, bananas, dried fruits and fresh vegetables.
**Potassium:** dried fruits, soya flour, molasses, wheatbran, raw salad vegetables, nuts, muesli, fresh fruit, cooked vegetables, wholemeal bread and flour, eggs,

cheese and brown rice.

**Zinc:** brewer's yeast, cheese, wholemeal bread, eggs, carrots, peanuts, rice, tomatoes, peas, sweetcorn.

The chart below compares 100g/4oz of various foods for fat, fibre, protein and calorie content.

### Microwave Cooking

Many people associate microwave cooking with convenience. A microwave oven is without doubt a time-saving appliance, but rather than being used purely to reheat convenience or ready-prepared foods, it can be used to make cooking fresh, healthy ingredients that much speedier and cleaner too. Many of the recipes in this book can be prepared either partly or totally with the help of a microwave oven. Instructions are given for use with a 650W oven; if you own an oven with a smaller or larger wattage, simply lengthen or shorten the cooking times accordingly.

### Freezing

As well as the obvious use of the freezer for storing surplus seasonal fresh fruits and vegetables, the freezer makes a perfect partner to the microwave oven in which ready made meals prepared with fresh seasonal produce can be thawed out quickly.

## ANIMAL VERSUS VEGETABLE FOODS per 100g/4oz

| | Fat (%) | Fibre(%) | Protein (%) | Calories |
|---|---|---|---|---|
| Beef | 24 | 0 | 16 | 280 |
| Chicken | 4 | 0 | 20 | 120 |
| Cod | 0.7 | 0 | 17 | 76 |
| Herring | 17 | 0 | 17 | 234 |
| Milk (whole) | 3.8 | 0 | 3.3 | 65 |
| Cheddar cheese | 33 | 0 | 26 | 406 |
| Eggs | 10 | 0 | 12 | 147 |
| Wholemeal flour | 2 | 9.6 | 13 | 318 |
| Brown rice | 1.9 | 0.9 | 7.5 | 360 |
| Haricot beans (raw weight) | 1.6 | 25 | 21 | 271 |
| Lentils (raw weight) | 1 | 11.7 | 23 | 304 |
| Walnuts (shelled weight) | 50 | 5 | 10 | 525 |

# SPRING

## MARCH · APRIL · MAY

Towards the end of spring the new vegetables of the season start to appear in plentiful supply. The beginning of spring however sees the last of winter's stored vegetables still in the shops; produce such as swedes, turnips, parsnips, leeks, old potatoes and carrots are still good value. As the weather warms up growth speeds up in the kitchen gardens and farms and fresh produce becomes available. New carrots, turnips, sprouting broccoli, spring greens and spinach eventually make way for the first English asparagus and new potatoes. Rhubarb becomes cheaper as the season progresses and forced produce is overtaken by outdoor varieties. Most of the fruit available is imported and citrus fruits, grapes and bananas are normally good buys now. Towards the end of May home-grown fruits start appearing, gooseberries normally coming first.

### SPRING MENUS

#### 1

*Citrus appetiser*

*Butter bean and mushroom Stroganoff with long-grain brown rice and lightly cooked carrots*

*Rhubarb crumble with yogurt*

#### 2

*Watercress soup with wholemeal croûtons*

*Vegetable biriani with spiced mushrooms*

*Fresh fruit*

#### 3

*French onion tartlets*

*Stir-fry vegetables with almonds and Chinese rice*

*Strained Greek-style natural yogurt*

Watercress soup (above); Mushroom soup; Spring vegetable soup

*Microwave note*

**Place the oil in a casserole with the onion and potato and cook for 2 minutes on maximum power. Add the mushrooms and heat for 2 minutes. Add the milk, stock and herbs and cook for 10 minutes, stirring after 5 minutes. Proceed as recipe.**

# MUSHROOM SOUP

## SERVES 4

*1 tablespoon sunflower oil*
*100 g/4 oz onion, chopped*
*100 g/4 oz potato, scrubbed and diced*
*275 g/10 oz button mushrooms, chopped*
*450 ml/¾ pint skimmed milk*
*450 ml/¾ pint vegetable stock*
*1 bay leaf*
*½ teaspoon dried thyme*
*freshly ground black pepper*
*chopped parsley to garnish (optional)*

■

*Preparation time **10 minutes***
*Cooking time **40 minutes***

**1** Heat the oil in a large saucepan. Stir in the onion and potato and cook over a low heat for 2 minutes without browning.
**2** Add the mushrooms to the pan, stirring in well and cook for a further minute. Stir in the skimmed milk, vegetable stock, bay leaf and thyme and bring to the boil. Reduce the heat and simmer gently for 30 minutes, until the vegetables are quite soft.
**3** Remove from heat and discard the bay leaf. Blend the soup in a liquidiser to a fine, smooth purée and reheat, seasoning with black pepper to taste. Serve, garnished with chopped parsley.

*The skimmed milk in this recipe gives a surprisingly creamy soup but contains far fewer calories and less fat than many recipes.*

# SPRING VEGETABLE SOUP

### SERVES 4

*75 g / 3 oz onion*
*100 g / 4 oz carrots (finger carrots are ideal)*
*100 g / 4 oz baby turnips*
*175 g / 6 oz cauliflower florets*
*100 g / 4 oz baby broad beans, or frozen peas, or frozen or fresh sweetcorn kernels*
*1 tablespoon sunflower oil*
*sprig of fresh thyme*
*1 bay leaf*
*900 ml / 1½ pints light vegetable stock*
*1 tablespoon chopped parsley*

*Preparation time **10 minutes***
*Cooking time **30 minutes***

■

**1** Finely chop the onion. Scrub the carrots and slice finely. Peel and dice the turnip.
**2** Heat the oil in a large saucepan and add the onion. Cook for 2 minutes before stirring in the carrot, turnip and cauliflower florets. Cook for 1 minute.
**3** Stir in the thyme, bay leaf and stock and bring to the boil. Add the frozen peas or sweetcorn if using. Bring to the boil and simmer for 20 minutes. Meanwhile, cook the broad beans or fresh sweetcorn kernels separately until tender and stir into the soup just before serving. Season to taste and pour into four soup bowls, garnished with freshly chopped parsley.

*A light, low-calorie soup, full of fibre and vitamins and low in fat.*

# WATERCRESS SOUP

### SERVES 4

*bunch of watercress, trimmed*
*15 g / ½ oz unsalted butter*
*100 g / 4 oz onion, chopped*
*100 g / 4 oz potato, scrubbed and diced*
*300 ml / ½ pint skimmed milk*
*600 ml / 1 pint vegetable stock*
*¼ teaspoon dried thyme*
*freshly ground black pepper*

■

*Preparation time **10 minutes***
*Cooking time **40 minutes***

■

**1** Reserve four watercress sprigs. Chop the remainder finely.
**2** Melt the butter in a large saucepan and add the onion. Cook gently for 2 minutes. Stir in the watercress and potato and cook for a further 2 minutes.
**3** Add remaining ingredients. Bring to the boil, reduce heat and simmer for 30 minutes.
**4** Blend in a liquidiser to a purée. Reheat. Garnish with reserved watercress sprigs.

*Watercress is a good source of minerals, especially of iron.*

---

**Mushroom soup**

*Per portion:*

Calories 110

Fat 4g

Fibre 3g

---

**Spring vegetable soup**

*Per portion:*

Calories 65

Fat 4g

Fibre 4g

---

**Watercress soup**

*Per portion:*

Calories 80

Fat 3g

Fibre 1g

---

*Microwave note*
**Cook the onion in the butter on full power for 2 minutes. Add the potato and watercress and cook for a further 3 minutes. Add the milk and stock and cook for 12 minutes on medium power. Proceed as recipe.**

**Microwave note**
At stage 2 cook the onions in the butter or margarine on full power for 3 minutes until soft.

| French onion tartlets | |
|---|---|
| **Per portion:** | |
| Calories | 420 |
| Fat | 25g |
| Fibre | 5g |

*French onion tartlet*

# FRENCH ONION TARTLETS

## SERVES 4

*175 g | 6 oz plain wholemeal flour*
*75 g | 3 oz soft vegetable margarine*
*generous pinch of mustard powder*
*cold water to mix*
### Filling
*175 g | 6 oz onion*
*15 g | ½ oz butter or soft vegetable margarine*
*175 g | 6 oz low-fat soft cheese*
*1 free-range egg*
*4 tablespoons skimmed milk*
*¼ teaspoon mustard powder*
*freshly ground black pepper*
*40 g | 1½ oz farmhouse Cheddar, finely grated*
*chopped chives to garnish*

■

*Preparation time* **10–15 minutes, plus 15 minutes to chill**
*Cooking time* **30 minutes**
*Oven temperature* **200 C, 400 F, gas 6**

**1** Sift the flour into a bowl and add the bran from the sieve. Rub in the margarine and stir in the mustard. Chill for 15 minutes. Add just sufficient cold water to mix to a soft dough and roll out the pastry to line four 10-cm/4-in tartlet tins. Bake blind (place a piece of greaseproof paper over the pastry and sprinkle over a few dried beans to prevent pastry bubbling up) for 10 minutes.
**2** Very finely chop the onion and cook gently in the butter or margarine without browning, until soft.
**3** Beat together the soft cheese, egg, milk, mustard and freshly ground black pepper.
**4** Remove the paper from the tartlet tins and divide the onion between the four tartlets. Pour over the beaten cheese mixture and sprinkle the grated Cheddar on top. Bake for 20 minutes and serve immediately while the tartlets are still light and fluffy. Garnish with chopped chives and serve with a light salad – finely shredded lettuce or Chinese leaves with finely shredded radicchio, form an attractive combination.

*A tasty hot starter, lower in calories than many conventional quiche recipes as low-fat soft cheese replaces the cream often used.*

*Russian dip and crudités; Citrus appetiser*

# RUSSIAN DIP AND CRUDITÉS

### SERVES 4

*100g/4oz low-fat soft cheese
4 tablespoons strained, Greek-style
natural yogurt
1 clove garlic, crushed
1 tablespoon tomato purée
dash of Tabasco or Worcestershire
sauce
freshly ground black pepper*
**To serve**
*carrots, cauliflower, peppers,
cucumber, celery*

∎

*Preparation time **15 minutes,
plus 4 hours, or overnight, to chill***

**1** Place the cheese in a bowl. Carefully stir in the yogurt, garlic, tomato purée and chosen sauce. Season with pepper. Cover tightly and leave to chill in the refrigerator for several hours, or overnight.
**2** Just before serving prepare the vegetables. Scrub the carrots and cut into fairly thick strips. Divide the cauliflower into florets, deseed the peppers and cut into fine strips, cut the cucumber and celery into strips.
**3** Serve the crudités with the dip.

*Choose a low-fat soft cheese such as continental quark as the base for the dip.*

# CITRUS APPETISER

### SERVES 4

*2 large oranges · 1 grapefruit
1 ugli fruit · juice of 1 lime
1 tablespoon Cointreau (optional)*

∎

*Preparation time **15 minutes, plus 30
minutes to chill***

∎

**1** Pare the rind from one orange.
**2** Peel the oranges, grapefruit and ugli fruit and remove pith. Cut into 2.5-cm/1-in lengths and toss together in the lime juice with the Cointreau, if using. Sprinkle with the pared orange rind. Chill for 30 minutes and serve.

*Citrus fruits are good value during spring and boost supplies of home-grown fruits, supplying valuable vitamin C.*

**Russian dip and crudités**

*Per portion:*

Calories 45

Fat 2g

Fibre 0g

**Citrus appetiser**

*Per portion:*

Calories 60

Fat trace

Fibre 2g

**Butter bean and mushroom Stroganoff**

| Per portion: | |
|---|---|
| Calories | 280 |
| Fat | 9g |
| Fibre | 15g |

*Butter bean and mushroom Stroganoff; Vegetable biriani*

*Microwave note*

**At stage 2, heat the onion on full power for 2 minutes. Add the mushrooms, cook for 1 minute. Add the flour and cook for 1 minute. Heat the milk with the stock, then beat into the mushroom mixture to form a smooth sauce. Cook for 2 minutes, stir in the butter beans, and reheat for 1 minute when the rice is ready. Stir in the yogurt and season to taste. Sprinkle with parsley.**

# BUTTER BEAN AND MUSHROOM STROGANOFF

## SERVES 4

*225 g/8 oz butter beans, soaked overnight*
*1 small onion, chopped*
*2 tablespoons sunflower oil*
*350 g/12 oz button mushrooms, halved*
*2 tablespoons wholemeal flour*
*175 ml/6 fl oz skimmed milk*
*175 ml/6 fl oz vegetable stock*
*$\frac{1}{4}$ teaspoon dried thyme*
*freshly ground black pepper*
*3 tablespoons natural yogurt*
*chopped parsley to garnish*

*Preparation time **10 minutes, plus overnight soaking***
*Cooking time **1 hour 25 minutes***

■

**1** Drain the beans and place in a pan of cold water and cook for 1–1$\frac{1}{4}$ hours or until quite tender.
**2** Cook the onion in the oil for 2 minutes.
**3** Add the mushrooms to the onion. Cook gently for 2 minutes. Stir in the flour and cook for 1 minute. Gradually add the milk and stock, stirring continuously to make a smooth sauce. Stir in the thyme and season to taste.
**4** Add the drained butter beans and reheat. Stir in the yogurt just before serving and sprinkle with the chopped parsley.

*A delicious and creamy supper dish, served with boiled, long-grain brown rice for a perfectly balanced protein intake.*

Preparation time **15 minutes**
Cooking time **30 minutes**

**1** Heat the oil in a large saucepan and add the cumin seeds. Let them sizzle for a few seconds, then add and cook the onion, garlic, potatoes and carrots gently together for 2 minutes.

**2** Add the turmeric and ground cumin and stir in well. Add the cauliflower florets and stir in. Now add the rice, mixing in the spice mixture thoroughly. Let this cook for 1 minute before adding the stock and bay leaf. Bring to the boil, then reduce the heat and simmer for 25 minutes.

**3** Toast the cashew nuts and almonds and have ready. Test the rice; if it is tender and all the stock is absorbed, then add the nuts and serve. If some stock still remains in the pan, then turn up the heat and cook uncovered for a while to evaporate the stock. Stir in the nuts and pepper to taste.

*A tasty way of livening up vegetables. The nuts complement the protein in the brown rice and add a delicious flavour too. Serve with Spiced mushrooms (see page 18) and some crunchy poppadums for a spicy Indian supper.*

*Microwave note*
**Cooking brown rice in a microwave does not save much time, but the microwave is invaluable in reheating cooked rice dishes such as this vegetable biriani. Either reheat the whole amount for 4–5 minutes, or serve on plates and reheat for a couple of minutes.**

# VEGETABLE BIRIANI

### SERVES 4

1 tablespoon sesame oil
½ teaspoon cumin seeds
100g/4oz onion, chopped
1 clove garlic, crushed
225g/8oz potatoes, scrubbed and diced
225g/8oz carrots, scrubbed and diced
½ teaspoon turmeric
½ teaspoon ground cumin
225g/8oz cauliflower florets
275g/10oz long-grain brown rice
750ml/1¼ pints vegetable stock
1 bay leaf
50g/2oz cashew nuts
50g/2oz split almonds
freshly ground black pepper

| Vegetable biriani | |
|---|---|
| **Per portion:** | |
| Calories 490 | |
| Fat 16g | |
| Fibre 10g | |

**Freezing note**
**Ready-made pancakes can be frozen for later use. Place each pancake on a layer of greaseproof paper and stack up. Place in a polythene bag and freeze.**

**Spinach-stuffed pancakes**

**Per portion:**

Calories 320

Fat 17g

Fibre 7g

# SPINACH-STUFFED PANCAKES

## SERVES 4

### Stuffing
*450g/1 lb spinach*
*100g/4oz low-fat soft cheese*
*50g/2oz onion, chopped*
*15g/½oz butter or 1 teaspoon sunflower oil*
*pinch of grated nutmeg*
*freshly ground black pepper*
### Batter
*100g/4oz plain wholemeal flour*
*1 free-range egg*
*300ml/½ pint skimmed milk*
*vegetable oil*
*75g/3oz toasted split almonds to garnish*

■

*Preparation time* **15 minutes**
*Cooking time* **25–30 minutes**

■

**1** Wash the spinach thoroughly, discarding any coarse stalks and yellowing leaves. Place in a saucepan and cook covered over a low heat for 5–8 minutes until soft. Drain thoroughly and chop. Mix with the cheese.
**2** Soften the onion in the butter or oil for 2 minutes. Mix into the spinach and cheese mixture with the nutmeg and enough pepper to taste.
**3** Make the pancakes. Sift the flour, adding any bran remaining in the sieve. Make a well in the centre and add the egg. Gradually mix in the flour, beating in half of the milk. Continue beating until really smooth. Mix in the remaining milk.
**4** Heat a little oil in an 18-cm/7-in crêpe pan. Tip in just enough mixture to coat the base of the pan and cook gently until set. Toss or turn to cook the other side. Cook all the batter in this way, keeping the pancakes hot on a plate.
**5** When all the batter has been used, place some of the spinach mixture in the centre of each pancake and fold or roll up. Place on an ovenproof plate and reheat all the pancakes together, either by placing, covered, in a moderate oven (180C, 350F, gas 4), or in a microwave on full power for 4 minutes.
**6** Just before serving, sprinkle with the toasted amonds.

*Pancakes can be made successfully with wholemeal flour and give a surprisingly light result. They make a useful 'container' for a savoury stuffing, such as this nutritious stuffing of spinach and low-fat soft cheese.*

# SPICED MUSHROOMS

## SERVES 4

*1 tablespoon sunflower oil*
*½ teaspoon ground coriander*
*½ teaspoon ground cumin*
*¼ teaspoon chilli powder (or half a fresh chilli, deseeded and chopped)*
*¼ teaspoon cayenne*
*¼ teaspoon turmeric*
*100g/4oz onion, chopped*
*2 cloves garlic, crushed*
*1 cm/½ in fresh root ginger, peeled and grated*
*350g/12oz button mushrooms*
*1 (425-g/15-oz) can or 450g/1 lb fresh tomatoes, peeled and chopped*

■

*Preparation time* **10 minutes**
*Cooking time* **30 minutes**

■

**1** Heat the oil and add the spices, onion, garlic and ginger. Cook for 2 minutes, then stir in the mushrooms and tomatoes. Bring to the boil, cover and simmer for 20 minutes. Serve hot.

*A delicious accompaniment to Vegetable biriani.*

| Spiced mushrooms | |
|---|---|
| *Per portion:* | |
| Calories **70** | |
| Fat **4g** | |
| Fibre **4g** | |

*Spiced mushrooms;
Spinach-stuffed
pancakes*

## Microwave note

**The tomato sauce, cheese sauce and spinach can all be cooked in the microwave oven to save time. The tomato sauce will need 8 minutes further cooking on full power after the onion, garlic and carrots have been cooked in the oil for 2 minutes on full power. The spinach will need 5–6 minutes in a roasting bag on full power and the cheese sauce can be prepared by melting the margarine on full power, stirring in the flour and cooking in the oven for 1 minute. Heat the milk for 2 minutes, then beat into the flour and margarine mixture. Cook for 2 minutes, stir in the cheese and pepper and cook for 1 further minute. The assembled lasagne could then be cooked on full power for 8 minutes.**

# LASAGNE BAKE

### SERVES 4

10 pieces wholemeal lasagne
100g/4oz onion, chopped
2 cloves garlic, crushed
1 tablespoon olive oil
175g/6oz carrots, finely diced
450g/1lb tomatoes, peeled and chopped
½ teaspoon dried or 1 teaspoon chopped fresh basil
1 red pepper, deseeded and chopped
1 bay leaf
450g/1lb spinach
25g/1oz soft vegetable margarine
25g/1oz plain wholemeal flour
300ml/½ pint skimmed milk
50g/2oz Cheddar cheese, finely grated, plus 15g/½oz
freshly ground black pepper

*Preparation time **35–40 minutes***
*Cooking time **1 hour 10 minutes***
*Oven temperature **190C, 375F, gas 5***

■

**1** Cook the lasagne by plunging the sheets into a pan of fast boiling water. Cook for 10–12 minutes until *al dente* (almost tender). Drain well.
**2** Make a tomato sauce. Cook the onion and garlic gently in the oil for 2 minutes. Add the carrots, tomatoes, basil, pepper and bay leaf. Bring to the boil, then reduce the heat and simmer for 25 minutes.
**3** Meanwhile, cook the spinach and chop finely, draining out surplus fluid.
**4** Make a cheese sauce. Melt the margarine in a pan. Stir in the flour and cook for 1 minute, before gradually adding the milk. Bring to the boil, stirring continuously to make a smooth sauce. Add the 50g/2oz of Cheddar and season with black pepper.
**5** Assemble the lasagne in a lightly oiled

oblong ovenproof dish by placing a layer of lasagne in the base and adding layers of tomato sauce, lasagne, spinach, tomato sauce and lasagne and finally topping with cheese sauce. Sprinkle with the remaining cheese and bake for 35 minutes or until brown and bubbling. Serve with green vegetables or a side salad.

*Wholemeal lasagne is higher in fibre and B vitamins than traditional white lasagne. Layer this tasty and nutritious pasta with iron-rich spinach instead of meat.*

# LENTIL SAUCE

### SERVES 4

*100g/4oz onion, chopped
2 celery sticks, sliced
2 cloves garlic, crushed
1 tablespoon olive oil
225g/8oz button mushrooms, sliced
1 red pepper, deseeded and chopped
1 green pepper, deseeded and chopped
200g/7oz red lentils
1 (425-g/15-oz) can or 450g/1lb fresh
tomatoes, peeled and chopped
½ teaspoon dried basil
2 bay leaves
300ml/½ pint dry red wine or vegetable
stock
2 tablespoons tomato purée
freshly ground black pepper
grated Parmesan cheese
chopped parsley to garnish*

■

*Preparation time* **15 minutes**
*Cooking time* **45 minutes**

■

**1** Cook the onion, celery and garlic in the oil for 2 minutes without browning.
**2** Stir in the mushrooms, peppers, lentils, tomatoes, basil, bay leaves, wine or stock and tomato purée. Bring to the boil, then reduce the heat, cover and simmer gently for 40 minutes, stirring occasionally to make sure the sauce does not stick; add a little extra stock if it begins to dry out. Season with freshly ground black pepper and serve stirred into cooked long-grain brown rice. Sprinkle over the Parmesan and garnish with parsley.

*A super vegetarian alternative to a traditional meat-based sauce. This can also be served with wholemeal spaghetti, or used as an alternative to the sauce in Lasagne bake (see page 20). Red wine gives a lovely rich flavour, but vegetable stock can be used in its place if preferred.*

(see page 20)

*Microwave note*
**The sauce can be cooked in the microwave. Cook the garlic, onion and celery in the oil for 1 minute on full power. Add the remaining ingredients, cover and cook for 15 minutes on full power. Stir and cook for a further 15 minutes until the lentils are fully soft.**

*Lasagne bake; Lentil sauce with rice*

| Lasagne bake | |
| --- | --- |
| *Per portion:* | |
| Calories 490 | |
| Fat 12g | |
| Fibre 17g | |

| Lentil sauce | |
| --- | --- |
| *Per portion:* | |
| Calories 400 | |
| Fat 7g | |
| Fibre 9g | |

*Stir-fry vegetables with almonds; Chinese rice*

**Stir-fry vegetables with almonds**

| | |
|---|---|
| **Per portion:** | |
| **Calories** 210 | |
| **Fat** 17g | |
| **Fibre** 8g | |

*Microwave note*

**It is possible to stir-fry in the microwave by using a preheated browning dish to start the dish off and cooking on full power until the vegetables are tender.**

# STIR-FRY VEGETABLES WITH ALMONDS

### SERVES 4

*2 leeks*
*100g/4oz carrots, scrubbed*
*100g/4oz swede, peeled*
*1 tablespoon sesame oil*
*2 cloves garlic, crushed*
*50g/2oz mushrooms, sliced*
*75g/3oz curly kale or other dark green leafy vegetable, shredded*
*1 tablespoon soy sauce*
*1 tablespoon dry sherry or rice wine*
*4 tablespoons water*
*225g/8oz mung beanshoots*
*100g/4oz split almonds, toasted*

*Preparation time **25 minutes***
*Cooking time **7 minutes***

■

**1** Trim away the coarse leaves and roots from the leeks, clean carefully and chop the leeks finely. Cut the carrots and swede into 2.5–5-cm/1–2-in long matchsticks.

**2** Heat the oil in a wok or large heavy-based frying pan. Add the garlic, leek, carrot and swede. Cook for 3 minutes, stirring often. Add the mushrooms and kale and cook for 1 minute. Add the soy sauce, sherry or rice wine, water and beanshoots. Cook for 3 minutes. Add the almonds and serve.

*Stir-frying is a quick method of cooking which helps to retain nutritional value. If you do not own a wok, a large heavy-based frying pan will do just as well.*

# CHINESE RICE

### SERVES 4

225g/8oz long-grain brown rice,
cooked and cooled
1 tablespoon sesame oil
100g/4oz mushrooms, finely sliced
100g/4oz beanshoots
1 large free-range egg

■

Preparation time **5 minutes**
Cooking time **10 minutes**

■

**1** The rice should be completely cool for
this dish, so refrigerate until required.
Separate the grains.
**2** Heat the oil in a wok or large, heavy-
based frying pan and add the rice. Stir in
thoroughly and cook for 4 minutes.
**3** Add the mushrooms and beanshoots
and cook for a further 2 minutes.
**4** Add the egg, stirring constantly to
break it up as it sets. Continue cooking
until it has set, then serve at once.

*Mushrooms and beanshoots are available
all the year round; neither depends on
the vagaries of the climate for growth as
each is raised under cover.*

# WALNUT AND SOFT CHEESE TAGLIATELLE

### SERVES 4

25g/1oz unsalted butter
100g/4oz onion, chopped
225g/8oz quark or similar low-fat soft
cheese
6 tablespoons strained, Greek-style
natural yogurt
1 tablespoon chopped fresh chives
freshly ground black pepper
350g/12oz wholemeal tagliatelle
100g/4oz walnut halves
1 tablespoon chopped fresh chives to
garnish

Preparation time **10 minutes**
Cooking time **10–20 minutes**

■

**1** Heat the butter and stir in the onion.
Cook over a low heat for 4 minutes.
**2** Remove from heat and stir in the quark
or soft cheese, yogurt and chives, then
season with pepper.
**3** Cook the tagliatelle in plenty of boiling
water for a couple of minutes, if using
fresh pasta, or for 12–15 minutes if using
dried pasta. Drain and return to the pan,
stirring in the sauce and walnut halves.
Heat through for a couple of minutes and
serve, garnished with chopped chives.

*Use a soft, low-fat cheese in preference to
fat-rich and calorie-laden cream cheeses
in this speedy supper dish. Butter gives a
richer taste to the sauce, but if preferred
a vegetable oil could be used in its place.*

| Chinese rice | |
|---|---|
| **Per portion:** | |
| **Calories 270** | |
| **Fat 6g** | |
| **Fibre 4g** | |

*Walnut and soft cheese
tagliatelle*

| Walnut and soft cheese tagliatelle | |
|---|---|
| **Per portion:** | |
| **Calories 580** | |
| **Fat 22g** | |
| **Fibre 10g** | |

# SUMMER

## JUNE · JULY · AUGUST

Summer months abound with fresh, colourful foods from both home and abroad. Soft fruit is at its prime, as strawberries, raspberries, red and blackcurrants, apricots, peaches and cherries fill greengrocers' shelves. Later in August the first English plums and blackberries become available. Fresh vegetables are just as plentiful, with traditional salad ingredients at their best now. Lettuces, cucumbers, tomatoes, spring onions and radishes are excellent value as are peppers, aubergines and, later in the season, courgettes, both home-grown and imported from Mediterranean countries. French, runner and broad beans are at their best, as are peas, summer cauliflower and cabbages. Corn-on-the-cob and marrows begin to appear towards the end of August.

### SUMMER MENUS

**1**

*Flageolets Niçoise*
*Mushroom moussaka with green salad*
*Strawberry choux puffs*

**2**

*Cucumber soup with wholemeal croûtons*
*Avocado risotto with mange-tout and tofu stir-fry*
*Fresh fruit salad with natural yogurt*

**3**

*Tomato and thyme soup*
*Ratatouille with Greek salad*
*Fresh fruit*

**Microwave note**
Place the oil, onion, celery and garlic in a large heatproof dish and cook on full power for 3 minutes. Stir in the remaining ingredients and cook for a further 15 minutes, stirring once.

**Tomato and thyme soup**

*Per portion:*

Calories 60

Fat 4g

Fibre 2g

**Cucumber soup**

*Per portion:*

Calories 100

Fat 4g

Fibre 2g

*Freezing note*
Like most soups, this soup freezes well, in a rigid airtight container or heavy duty polythene bag. Thaw at room temperature rather than in the microwave as the soup is to be served cold.

# TOMATO AND THYME SOUP

### SERVES 4

1 tablespoon olive oil
100g/4oz onion, chopped
½ celery stick, chopped
1 clove garlic, crushed
450g/1lb tomatoes, peeled and chopped
1 red pepper, deseeded and chopped
450ml/¾ pint vegetable stock
½ teaspoon chopped fresh thyme
1 bay leaf
freshly ground black pepper

■

Preparation time **20 minutes**
Cooking time **35 minutes**

■

**1** Heat the oil and cook the onion, celery and garlic over a low heat for 2 minutes.
**2** Add the tomatoes, pepper, stock, thyme and bay leaf. Bring to the boil, cover and reduce heat. Simmer for 30 minutes. Remove bay leaf, season with pepper and serve.

*This is a light, low-calorie, refreshing soup. A good lunch dish or starter. Serve with either fresh wholemeal bread or wholemeal croûtons.*

# CUCUMBER SOUP

### SERVES 4

100g/4oz onion, chopped
100g/4oz potato, peeled and chopped
1 tablespoon sunflower oil
275g/10oz cucumber, peeled and diced
300ml/½ pint skimmed milk
300ml/½ pint vegetable stock
1 bay leaf
250ml/8fl oz natural yogurt
freshly ground black pepper
freshly chopped chives to garnish

Preparation time **15–20 minutes**
Cooking time **25 minutes**

■

**1** Cook the onion and potato in the oil for 2 minutes. Add the cucumber and cook for 1 minute. Add the milk, stock and bay leaf. Bring to the boil, reduce heat and simmer for 20 minutes until the vegetables are quite soft.
**2** Discard the bay leaf and blend the soup in a liquidiser. Stir in the yogurt, reserving 2 tablespoons. Leave to cool and season to taste with pepper. Divide between four serving bowls and garnish with the remaining yogurt and chives.

*Low in calories, this refreshing summer soup looks pretty when served garnished with a swirl of natural yogurt and chives.*

*Spinach and avocado salad (above);
Cucumber soup;
Tomato and thyme soup*

# SPINACH AND AVOCADO SALAD

## SERVES 4

*450 g/1 lb young spinach leaves
3 tablespoons olive oil
1 clove garlic, crushed
1 tablespoon fresh lemon juice
freshly ground black pepper
50 g/2 oz sunflower seeds
2 ripe avocados*

■

*Preparation time 15 minutes
Cooking time 2–3 minutes*

■

**1** Gently tear the spinach leaves away from the stalks and tear into small shreds. Place in a bowl.

**2** In a screw-topped jar shake together the oil, garlic and lemon juice with a dash of freshly ground black pepper. Pour over the spinach and toss thoroughly.
**3** Lightly toast the sunflower seeds for 2–3 minutes either under a very hot grill or in a heavy-based frying pan. Set aside.
**4** Cut the avocados in half and remove the stones. Cut the flesh away from the skin and slice thinly. Arrange on top of the spinach in the bowl. Toss the sunflower seeds on top, and serve at once.

*The mixture of spinach and avocado is delightful. Make sure the avocados are quite ripe and the spinach tender.*

| Spinach and avocado salad | |
|---|---|
| **Per portion:** | |
| Calories 440 | |
| Fat 40g | |
| Fibre 10g | |

| Flageolets Niçoise |
| --- |
| *Per portion:* |
| Calories 300 |
| Fat 13g |
| Fibre 13g |

*Flageolets Niçoise*

# FLAGEOLETS NIÇOISE

### SERVES 4

*225 g / 8 oz flageolet beans, soaked*
*1 clove garlic, peeled*
*4 large ripe tomatoes*
*1 large red pepper*
*12 black olives*
*2 tablespoons olive oil*
*1 tablespoon white wine vinegar*
*1 tablespoon chopped parsley*
*1 tablespoon chopped chives*
*2 hard-boiled, free-range eggs, chopped*
*freshly ground black pepper*

■

Preparation time **20 minutes, plus overnight soaking**
Cooking time **1¼ hours**

**1** Drain the beans, place in saucepan of cold water and cook for 1–1¼ hours or until tender. Drain.
**2** Rub the garlic clove around the inside of the bowl you will be serving the salad in. Chop the tomatoes. Deseed and chop the pepper and stone the olives.
**3** Place the oil and vinegar with the parsley and chives in a clean screw-topped jar. As soon as the beans are cooked, shake the dressing ingredients together and pour over the beans. Stir in the egg, tomatoes, pepper and olives and place in the salad bowl. Season with pepper and serve when the beans have cooled.

*More expensive than other dried beans the flageolet bean should be reserved for special dishes, like this attractive and flavourful salad; perfect for warm summer days, served as a light first course, or as an accompaniment.*

*Mushroom moussaka*

# MUSHROOM MOUSSAKA

## SERVES 4

450g/1 lb aubergine
sea salt
150ml/¼ pint tomato juice
1 tablespoon olive oil
100g/4oz onion, chopped
2 cloves garlic, crushed
350g/12oz button mushrooms, sliced
1 red pepper, deseeded and chopped
450g/1 lb tomatoes, peeled and
chopped
½ teaspoon dried or 1 teaspoon
chopped fresh marjoram
1 bay leaf
3 free-range eggs
300ml/½ pint natural yogurt
freshly ground black pepper
50g/2oz farmhouse Cheddar cheese,
finely grated

■

Preparation time **45 minutes**
Cooking time **75 minutes**
Oven temperature **190 C, 375 F, gas 5**

**1** Cut the aubergine into 5-mm/¼-in thick slices, sprinkle with sea salt and leave to stand for 30 minutes. Rinse and wipe dry. (This process removes some of the bitterness of the aubergine.)
**2** Poach the aubergine slices in the tomato juice for 3 minutes each side. Set aside.
**3** Heat the oil in a separate pan and cook the onion and garlic gently for 2 minutes. Stir in the mushrooms, pepper and tomatoes and any extra juice remaining from the pan used to poach the aubergine. If using dried marjoram add to the pan with a bay leaf. Bring to the boil, then reduce heat and simmer for 20 minutes. If using fresh marjoram, add at this stage.
**4** Place a layer of aubergine in a lightly oiled ovenproof dish, top with a layer of sauce, add remaining aubergines and finish with the remaining sauce. In a jug beat together the eggs and yogurt with pepper and pour on top.
**5** Sprinkle with the grated cheese and bake for 30–40 minutes. Serve at once.

*A rich vegetable and mushroom sauce replaces the lamb usually used in this traditional Greek dish. To cut down on fat, the aubergine is cooked in tomato juice rather than oil.*

*Microwave note*
**The entire dish could be prepared in the microwave to save time. Poach the aubergine slices on full power for 2 minutes each side. Heat the onion and garlic in the oil on full power for 2 minutes, add the tomatoes, mushrooms, herbs and pepper and cook on full power for 8 minutes. Layer the aubergine with sauce, top with the egg and yogurt mixture and cook on full power for 5 minutes. Add the cheese and cook for a further minute to melt the cheese.**

| Avocado risotto |
| --- |
| **Per portion:** |
| Calories 480 |
| Fat 18g |
| Fibre 7g |

| Courgette soufflé quiche |
| --- |
| **Per portion:** |
| Calories 330 |
| Fat 21g |
| Fibre 4g |

*Microwave note*
**The sauce could be made in advance, but do not add the avocado until just before serving. Reheat in the microwave on full power for 3 minutes, stir and heat for a further 3 minutes. Proceed as recipe from stage 3.**

# AVOCADO RISOTTO

### SERVES 4

*100g/4oz onion, chopped*
*2 cloves garlic, crushed*
*1 tablespoon olive oil*
*450g/1 lb tomatoes, peeled and chopped*
*225g/8oz mushrooms, halved*
*150ml/¼ pint dry white wine*
*1 teaspoon chopped fresh or ½ teaspoon dried basil*
*275g/10oz long-grain brown rice*
*1 large or 2 small avocados*
*freshly ground black pepper*
*freshly grated Parmesan cheese to serve*

■

*Preparation time **10 minutes***
*Cooking time **30 minutes***

■

**1** Cook the onion and garlic in the oil over a low heat for 2 minutes. Add the tomatoes, mushrooms, wine and dried basil, if using. Bring to the boil, reduce the heat and simmer for 20 minutes.
**2** Meanwhile place the rice in a pan with enough cold water to cover. Bring to the boil, then reduce to a steady simmer and cook for 25 minutes or until the rice is tender.
**3** Cut the avocado(s) in half and remove the stone(s). Slice the flesh and add to the sauce with the fresh basil, if using, and freshly ground black pepper to taste. Heat through while the rice nears the end of its cooking time.
**4** Drain the rice and arrange on the serving plates. Pour the sauce into the centre of the rice and serve at once, with freshly grated Parmesan.

*Avocados are rarely served hot, but this special risotto includes warm avocado. For the special effect in the picture, cook an additional 175g/6oz rice, place in a 20-cm/8-in ring tin and bake for 5 minutes in a moderately hot oven (200C, 400F, gas 6) before turning out and serving the sauce in the centre.*

# COURGETTE SOUFFLÉ QUICHE

### SERVES 4

***Pastry***
*100g/4oz plain wholemeal flour*
*50g/2oz soft vegetable margarine*
*cold water to mix*
***Filling***
*175g/6oz courgettes, chopped*
*20g/¾oz soft vegetable margarine*
*20g/¾oz plain wholemeal flour*
*150ml/¼ pint skimmed milk*
*freshly ground black pepper*
*40g/1½oz farmhouse Cheddar cheese, finely grated*
*2 free-range eggs*

■

*Preparation time **35 minutes, plus 20 minutes to chill***
*Cooking time **35 minutes***
*Oven temperature **200C, 400F, gas 6***

■

**1** Sift the flour into a mixing bowl, adding the bran from the sieve. Rub in the margarine until the mixture resembles fine breadcrumbs. Chill for 20 minutes. Add just sufficient cold water to mix to a soft dough. Roll out on a lightly floured surface to a circle just larger than an 18-cm/7-in flan dish or ring, line and bake blind for 10 minutes.
**2** Steam or cook the courgettes in a little boiling water for 5 minutes. Drain.
**3** Melt the margarine in a saucepan and stir in the flour. Cook for 1 minute, then gradually add the milk, beating constantly. Bring to the boil to let the sauce thicken. Season and stir in the Cheddar.
**4** Separate the eggs and beat the egg yolks into the sauce. Add the courgettes. Whisk the egg whites until they stand in stiff peaks and using a metal tablespoon, fold a little of the mixture into the sauce, then carefully fold in the remainder. Pour into the baked pastry case and bake for 20 minutes until the mixture is just firm to the touch and golden brown.

*Serve this impressive quiche as soon as it is cooked, before it collapses.*

*Avocado risotto;
Courgette soufflé
quiche*

*Microwave note*

**Bake the pastry case
blind in the microwave
on full power for 4
minutes. Remove the
paper and continue to
cook for 1 minute. The
sauce can also be
prepared in the
microwave. Melt the
margarine on full
power for 1 minute.
Add the flour and cook
for 1 minute. Heat the
milk on full power for
2 minutes, then stir
into the flour roux.
Return to the
microwave for a
further 2 minutes to
cook. Season and stir in
the Cheddar. Proceed
from stage 4 of
Courgette soufflé quiche.**

## Microwave note

The dish can be prepared in 20 minutes in the microwave, but I find the flavours develop better by cooking on the hob for a longer period of time. It is, however, useful to start the dish off in the microwave. Heat the oil, onion and garlic on full power for 2 minutes. Stir in the diced aubergines, return to the microwave for a further 2 minutes. Then transfer to a saucepan and proceed, adding the remaining ingredients.

*Ratatouille*

| Ratatouille | |
|---|---|
| **Per portion:** | |
| **Calories 100** | |
| **Fat 8g** | |
| **Fibre 3g** | |

## Freezing note

Freeze in rigid containers. Defrost at room temperature or on defrost setting in the microwave for 15 minutes plus 5 minutes standing time.

# RATATOUILLE

### SERVES 4

*225 g | 8 oz aubergine*
*2 tablespoons olive oil*
*100 g | 4 oz onion, chopped*
*2 cloves garlic, crushed*
*225 g | 8 oz courgettes, sliced*
*1 green pepper, deseeded and sliced*
*1 red pepper, deseeded and sliced*
*450 g | 1 lb tomatoes, peeled and chopped*
*½ teaspoon dried or 2 teaspoons fresh chopped basil*

■

*Preparation time* **15 minutes**
*Cooking time* **50 minutes**

**1** Cut the aubergine into 1-cm/½-in cubes.

**2** Heat the oil in a large saucepan. Add the onion and garlic and cook for 2 minutes without browning. Add the aubergine and cook for a further 2 minutes. Add the dried basil, if using, and remaining ingredients, slowly bring to the boil, cover with a tight-fitting lid, reduce the heat and simmer for 45 minutes. Add the fresh basil 5 minutes before the end of cooking. Season with pepper. Serve hot or chilled.

*When Mediterranean vegetables are so cheap in the summer months, make batches of ratatouille and freeze for use on dull winter days. Fresh basil gives the best flavour, but dried can be used in its place. Add dried basil with the tomatoes to let the flavour develop; fresh basil should be added near the end of cooking.*

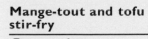

# MANGE-TOUT AND TOFU STIR-FRY

## SERVES 4

*450 g/1 lb tofu*
*225 g/8 oz mange-tout peas*
*2 spring onions*
*1 tablespoon sesame oil*
*1 clove garlic, crushed*
*2 tablespoons vegetable stock*
*2 teaspoons soy sauce*
*2 teaspoons dry sherry or rice wine*

■

*Preparation time **20 minutes***
*Cooking time **5 minutes***

**1** Squeeze out gently any excess moisture from the tofu in a clean tea-towel. Unwrap and cut into 1-cm/½-in cubes.
**2** Wash the mange-tout peas and trim any stalks. Trim away the roots and coarse leaves from the spring onions, cut in half and then slice lengthwise into four.
**3** Heat the oil in a wok or large frying pan. Add the garlic and heat for 2 minutes. Add the mange-tout peas and tofu and coat in the oil. Heat for 1 minute. Add the stock, soy sauce and sherry or rice wine and cook for a further 2 minutes, stirring well. Add the spring onions, stir in and serve at once.

*Tofu is a versatile low-calorie, low-fat food which is made from soya beans. Lacking in any distinct flavour of its own, tofu lends itself to a whole variety of both savoury and sweet dishes.*

| Mange-tout and tofu stir-fry | |
| --- | --- |
| *Per portion:* | |
| Calories | 150 |
| Fat | 0g |
| Fibre | 2g |

*Mange-tout and tofu stir-fry*

**Pipérade**

| Per portion: | |
|---|---|
| Calories | 180 |
| Fat | 13g |
| Fibre | 1g |

*Stuffed peppers;*
*Pipérade*

## Microwave note

**The microwave cooks scrambled eggs quickly. The entire dish can be prepared on full power. Heat the onion, garlic and butter or oil for 2 minutes. Add the pepper, tomatoes and cook for 2 minutes. Add the eggs and cook for 2 minutes. Stir well and cook for a further 3 minutes or until set.**

# PIPÉRADE

### SERVES 4

*25 g/1 oz butter or 1 tablespoon olive oil*
*50 g/2 oz onion, chopped*
*1 clove garlic, crushed*
*1 green pepper, deseeded and chopped*
*6 free-range eggs, beaten*
*freshly ground black pepper*
*225 g/8 oz tomatoes, peeled and chopped*
*pinch of chilli powder*
*chopped parsley to garnish*

*Preparation time **10 minutes***
*Cooking time **7 minutes***

■

**1** Heat the butter or oil in a saucepan and cook the onion, garlic and pepper for 2 minutes.
**2** Season the eggs with pepper, stir into the pan and cook over a low heat, stirring constantly, for 3 minutes.
**3** Add the tomatoes and chilli powder, and cook for a further 2 minutes or until the eggs are set. Serve at once, garnished with chopped parsley.

*This Mediterranean dish transforms scrambled egg into a nutritious lunch.*

# STUFFED PEPPERS

### SERVES 4

*100 g/4 oz haricot beans, soaked overnight*
*100 g/4 oz onion, chopped*
*2 cloves garlic, crushed*
*1 tablespoon olive oil*
*450 g/1 lb fresh tomatoes, peeled and chopped*
*100 g/4 oz mushrooms, sliced*
*½ teaspoon dried or 1 teaspoon chopped fresh basil*
*4 red or green medium peppers*
*75 g/3 oz farmhouse Cheddar cheese, grated*
*3 tablespoons sunflower seeds*

■

*Preparation time* **10 minutes, plus overnight soaking**
*Cooking time* **2 hours 10 minutes**

■

**1** Drain the beans and cook for 1–1½ hours in a pan of water until soft; alternatively pressure cook for 10 minutes at 6.75-kg/ 15-lb pressure. Drain.
**2** Cook the onion and garlic in the oil for 2 minutes. Stir in the tomatoes, mushrooms and dried basil, if using, and bring to the boil. Reduce the heat and simmer for 20 minutes; add fresh basil at this stage, if using. Stir in the beans and simmer for a further 5 minutes.
**3** Cut the peppers in half lengthwise, deseed and blanch in a pan of boiling water for 2 minutes. Drain thoroughly and arrange in a shallow flameproof dish. Fill each half with the sauce. Scatter the cheese on top of the peppers with the sunflower seeds. Place under a hot grill for 4–5 minutes until the topping is golden and bubbling. Serve at once.

*This unusual filling combines haricot beans with the best of summer's fresh produce in a nutritious supper dish. Serve with wholemeal pasta.*

| Stuffed peppers | |
|---|---|
| **Per portion:** | |
| Calories 280 | |
| Fat 15g | |
| Fibre 10g | |

*Microwave note*
**The sauce can be prepared using the microwave. At stage 2, place the onion, garlic and oil in a covered casserole dish on full power and cook for 2 minutes. Add the tomatoes, mushrooms and dried basil and cook for a further 5 minutes. Add the beans and cook for a further 2 minutes. Then place the blanched peppers, filled and topped with cheese and sunflower seeds in the microwave on full power for 3 minutes. Serve at once.**

Paella

_Per portion:_

Calories 340

Fat 8g

Fibre 7g

# PAELLA

## SERVES 4

225 g/8 oz French beans
2 tablespoons olive oil
175 g/6 oz onion, chopped
2 cloves garlic, crushed
225 g/8 oz tomatoes, peeled and
chopped
generous pinch of turmeric or saffron
225 g/8 oz mushrooms, sliced
275 g/10 oz long-grain brown rice
600 ml/1 pint vegetable stock plus
150 ml/$\frac{1}{4}$ pint dry cider (or use all
vegetable stock)
freshly ground black pepper

■

Preparation time **10 minutes**
Cooking time **35 minutes**

■

**1** Trim the beans and cut into 1-cm/$\frac{1}{2}$-in lengths.
**2** Place the oil in a paella pan or large frying pan with a lid or in a large heavy-based saucepan. Stir in the onions, garlic and tomatoes, and cook gently for 5 minutes, covered.
**3** Add the turmeric and mushrooms, stirring in thoroughly. Cook for 1 minute. Add the rice and stir in well and cook for a further minute, before adding the stock, cider, if using, and beans. Bring to the boil, cover and reduce the heat. Let the mixture simmer for 25 minutes without disturbing. Test the rice to see if it is cooked. If the rice is ready and some liquid remains, then turn up the heat and cook to evaporate; if the rice is not cooked, cover again and let it cook gently until the grains are quite tender. Season to taste with black pepper and serve at once.

_Paella is usually associated with shellfish and chicken, but traditional farmhouse-style paella is served without fish or poultry in a similar fashion to this recipe._

_Freezing and Microwave note_
**Paella can be frozen either in a rigid, airtight container or in a polythene bag, sealed. Defrost in the microwave for 20 minutes, then turn up to full power and reheat for 8 minutes.**

# KEBABS

## SERVES 4

225 g/8 oz aubergine
sea salt
225 g/8 oz courgettes
1 red pepper, deseeded
1 green pepper, deseeded
2 small onions
8 button mushrooms
juice of $\frac{1}{2}$ lemon
3 tablespoons olive oil
freshly ground black pepper
$\frac{1}{2}$ teaspoon dried or 1 teaspoon
chopped fresh marjoram (optional)
1 clove garlic, crushed (optional)

*Paella; Kebabs*

*Preparation time* **45 minutes**
*Cooking time* **20 minutes**

∎

**1** Slice the aubergine into 1-cm/$\frac{1}{2}$-in rings and sprinkle with salt. Leave for 30 minutes to draw out the bitterness. Pat dry and cut into cubes.

**3** Cut the courgettes and peppers into 1-cm/$\frac{1}{2}$-in slices. Quarter the onions. Wipe the mushrooms.

**3** Thread the prepared vegetables on to four long or eight short skewers.

**4** Mix together the lemon juice, olive oil, pepper, marjoram and garlic, if using. Baste the kebabs with this mixture just before cooking on a barbecue or under a hot grill, and baste at frequent intervals during cooking too. Allow 10–20 minutes to cook, turning the skewers to ensure even cooking.

*The flavour is best if the kebabs are cooked over a barbecue, but the recipe still works well when cooked under a hot grill.*

| Kebabs | |
|---|---|
| *Per portion:* | |
| Calories | 140 |
| Fat | 11g |
| Fibre | 3g |

| Pesto | |
|---|---|
| *Per portion:* | |
| Calories 210 | |
| Fat 23g | |
| Fibre 0g | |

# PESTO

### SERVES 4

*12 basil sprigs*
*1 clove garlic*
*4 tablespoons grated Parmesan cheese*
*1 tablespoon pine nuts*
*4–5 tablespoons olive oil*

■

Preparation time **25 minutes**

■

**1** Wash the basil, pat dry and strip the leaves from the stems. Place the leaves in a pestle and mortar with the garlic and crush together until smooth.
**2** Gradually add the cheese and pine nuts, working up a paste, with the oil. The texture should be thick and creamy,

rather like mayonnaise. Pesto is best served freshly made with cooked wholemeal pasta. These days, it is possible to buy fresh pasta, rather than dried, from many supermarkets and specialist delicatessens and this gives a more authentic dish.

*Traditionally a pestle and mortar is used to mix this fragrant sauce, but a liquidiser can also be used. Fresh basil is an essential ingredient as is fresh Parmesan cheese.*

*Greek salad; Pesto with wholemeal fresh pasta; Green salad (below)*

# GREEK SALAD

### SERVES 4

*450g/1 lb ripe tomatoes, sliced
1 small onion, sliced into rings
½ cucumber, sliced
225g/8oz feta cheese, diced
100g/4oz black olives, stoned
1 teaspoon chopped fresh basil
3 tablespoons olive oil
1 teaspoon lemon juice*

■

*Preparation time* **15 minutes**

■

**1** Place the tomato, onion and cucumber in a bowl.
**2** Arrange the cheese and olives on top of the salad.

**3** Shake the basil, olive oil and lemon juice together and pour over the salad. Serve at once.

*Feta cheese adds the distinctive flavour to this bright and colourful summer salad.*

# GREEN SALAD

### SERVES 4

*1 large Cos or Webb's Wonder lettuce
or 2 small round lettuces
2 bunches of watercress
box of mustard and cress or alfalfa
sprouts, or 100g/4oz mung
beansprouts
½ cucumber, sliced
1 green pepper, deseeded and sliced
4 spring onions, chopped
1 tablespoon white wine vinegar or
cider vinegar
3 tablespoons olive or sunflower oil
pinch of mustard powder
freshly ground black pepper
1 tablespoon chopped chives or parsley*

■

*Preparation time* **20 minutes**

■

**1** Wash the lettuce well, removing any coarse or yellowing leaves. Cut the leaves into smaller pieces if using Cos or Webb's Wonder. Place in a salad bowl.
**2** Trim any yellowing leaves from the watercress. Add to the bowl. Trim the roots from the mustard and cress, if using. Add to the bowl, or add the beansprouts.
**3** Add the cucumber, pepper and spring onion.
**4** In a screw-topped jar, shake together the vinegar, oil, mustard, pepper and chives or parsley. Pour over the salad and toss together thoroughly. Serve at once as the leaves soon go soggy in the dressing.

*There is nothing more attractive than a fresh, crispy green salad served on a warm summer's day. Take the trouble to add more interesting 'greenery' for a more exciting taste. Don't forget watercress either as it is an excellent source of iron and B vitamins.*

| Greek salad | | |
| --- | --- | --- |
| *Per portion:* | | |
| Calories 260 | | |
| Fat 18g | | |
| Fibre 3g | | |

| Green salad | | |
| --- | --- | --- |
| *Per portion:* | | |
| Calories 120 | | |
| Fat 11g | | |
| Fibre 2g | | |

*Strawberry choux puffs*

**Strawberry choux puffs**

*Per portion:*

Calories 260

Fat 14g

Fibre 2g

**Raspberry choux puffs**

*Per portion:*

Calories 260

Fat 14g

Fibre 5g

*Freezing note*

**Choux pastry can be frozen successfully. Leave the puffs to cool before placing in a strong polythene bag, securing tightly and freezing. Defrost at room temperature.**

# STRAWBERRY CHOUX PUFFS

### SERVES 4

*150 ml/¼ pint water*
*50 g/2 oz soft vegetable margarine*
*65 g/2½ oz 85% plain wheatmeal flour, sifted*
*2 free-range eggs*
*225 g/8 oz strawberries or raspberries*
*350 ml/12 fl oz strained, Greek-style yogurt*

■

*Preparation time* **25 minutes**
*Cooking time* **25 minutes**
*Oven temperature* **220 C, 425 F, gas 7**
**190 C, 375 F, gas 5**

■

**1** Place the water and margarine in a large saucepan and heat gently. When the margarine has melted turn up the heat and let the mixture come to the boil. Quickly add the flour, beat in and remove from heat. Continue to beat until the mixture is smooth and glossy and leaves the sides of the pan without sticking.

**2** Cool slightly. Beat in one egg thoroughly and when it has been totally mixed in, add the second and beat thoroughly.
**3** Place heaped teaspoonsful of the mixture on to two lightly oiled baking trays and bake for 15 minutes. Then reduce the oven temperature and cook for a further 10 minutes or until the pastry is completely cooked. Test by pressing the sides of the puffs; if they give, they need a little longer. When quite firm to the touch, remove from the oven and slit the side of each puff to let the steam escape; return to the oven to finally dry out for a further 5 minutes. Place on wire racks and leave to cool completely.
**4** Hull the fruit and chop roughly, reserving a few whole strawberries or raspberries for decoration. Mix with the yogurt and use this mixture to fill the puffs. Pile up on a plate, decorating with the reserved fruit, halved if using strawberries.

*A delicious version of that favourite dessert, profiteroles; calorie-rich chocolate sauce is replaced with fresh strawberries or raspberries. Greek yogurt is used in place of the cream.*

# FRESH FRUIT SALAD

### SERVES 4

*½ honeydew melon · 2 oranges*
*100 g/4 oz white grapes*
*100 g/4 oz black grapes*
*2 peaches or nectarines*
*1 tablespoon Cointreau (optional)*
*3 tablespoons apple or orange juice*
*2 red-skinned dessert apples*
*juice of ½ lemon · 1 banana*
*1 kiwi fruit (optional)*

■

*Preparation time* **25 minutes, plus 3 hours to chill (optional)**

■

**1** Cut the flesh of the melon away from the skin and remove the seeds. Dice and place in a large glass bowl, with any juice.

*Fresh fruit salad*

**2** Peel the orange and remove any pith. Cut into segments and cut each segment in four. Add to the bowl, with any juice.
**3** Halve the grapes and remove the pips. Add the grapes to the bowl. Cut the peaches or nectarines in half, remove the stones and chop the flesh. Add to the bowl with the Cointreau, if using, and apple or orange juice. Mix thoroughly, cover and chill if liked, for up to 3 hours. Alternatively proceed at once and omit the chilling stage.
**4** Cut the apples into quarters, remove the core and either slice finely or dice the flesh. Toss in the lemon juice. Peel the banana and slice thinly. Add to the apples and then to the bowl. Finally, peel the kiwi fruit, if using, slice thinly, halve slices

and arrange on top of the fruit salad.

*The most versatile of all desserts, fresh fruit salad can be varied according to the fruit available; it can be an inexpensive dish for an everyday dessert using cheap fresh fruits, or can be transformed into something more exotic with the addition of some more unusual tropical fruit such as mangoes, guavas and papaya. Adding a tablespoon of a light liqueur such as Cointreau and leaving the fruit to marinate for an hour, gives a superb tasting dessert. Use freshly pressed apple juice rather than concentrate. Offer natural yogurt for a lighter accompaniment than fat-rich cream.*

| Fresh fruit salad | |
|---|---|
| *Per portion:* | |
| Calories 160 | |
| Fat 0g | |
| Fibre 6g | |

# AUTUMN

## SEPTEMBER · OCTOBER · NOVEMBER

Autumn is a season of contrast in fresh foods: September sees plums, damsons, blackberries and greengages at their best with the new season's apples and pears arriving in quick succession as the month progresses. By the end of November, however, it is the imported satsumas, clementines and oranges which are best value. Summer's courgettes, marrows and corn-on-the-cob are plentiful in early autumn, but by the end of the season the first of winter's root crops – swedes, carrots, turnips and parsnips – are best value and in plentiful supply. Cabbages and cauliflower are also good value now and Brussels sprouts also come into season at this time.

### AUTUMN MENUS

**I**

*Waldorf salad with hot wholemeal bread*

*Swede and leek roulade with roast potatoes and carrots*

*Fresh fruit*

**2**

*Pears with soft cheese and almonds*

*Cannellini goulash with long-grain brown rice and broccoli*

*Baked apples with yogurt*

**3**

*Rosy beet soup*

*Hazelnut-stuffed marrow*

*Fresh fruit*

# APPLE AND STILTON POPOVERS

## SERVES 4

### Pastry
175 g/6 oz plain wholemeal flour
75 g/3 oz soft vegetable margarine
cold water to mix

### Filling
50 g/2 oz onion, grated
225 g/8 oz cooking apple, peeled, cored and grated
75 g/3 oz Stilton cheese, grated

### Glaze
1 free-range egg, beaten
1 tablespoon sesame seeds

■

Preparation time **30 minutes, plus 15 minutes to chill**

Cooking time **20 minutes**
Oven temperature **200 C, 400 F, gas 6**

■

**1** Sift the flour into a mixing bowl and add the bran from the sieve. Rub in the margarine until the mixture resembles fine breadcrumbs. Place the bowl in the refrigerator to rest for 15 minutes.

**2** Mix together the onion, apple and Stilton.

**3** Add just enough cold water to the flour and margarine mixture to mix to a soft dough. Divide into four. Roll out each quarter on a lightly floured surface and cut out a 13-cm/5-in circle. Dampen the edges with a pastry brush and divide the filling between the four circles, placing on one half of the circle and folding the remaining half over. Seal the edges and flute with a knife. Make three slits to let the steam escape. Place on a baking tray, then glaze with the egg and scatter sesame seeds on top.

**4** Bake for 15–20 minutes.

Apple and Stilton
popovers; Pears with
soft cheese and almonds

Stilton is a cheese to be reserved for special occasions – not only is it quite expensive, but it is also one of the fattiest cheeses. However, with its rich flavour a little goes a long way as in this unusual first course. Serve with a salad garnish.

# PEARS WITH SOFT CHEESE AND ALMONDS

## SERVES 4

4 small or 2 large ripe Comice pears
100 g/4 oz low-fat soft cheese
25 g/1 oz ground almonds
50 g/2 oz flaked almonds
shredded lettuce

*Preparation time **15 minutes***
*Cooking time **30 minutes***

■

**1** Wipe the pears and halve. Remove the cores.
**2** Blend the soft cheese with the ground almonds and pile into the cavities of the pears. Arrange on a bed of shredded lettuce.
**3** Toast the flaked almonds for 2–3 minutes under a hot grill and sprinkle on top of the pears. Serve at once, before the pears have a chance to brown.

*Few people consider serving pears as a first course, but this recipe makes a really attractive starter. Choose home-grown, plump Comice pears for best results.*

**Pears with soft cheese and almonds**

| *Per portion:* |
| --- |
| Calories 160 |
| Fat 12g |
| Fibre 4g |

# PUMPKIN SOUP

## SERVES 4

*450g/1 lb pumpkin*
*1 tablespoon sunflower oil*
*100g/4oz onion, chopped*
*½ teaspoon ground cumin*
*pinch of cayenne*
*450ml/¾ pint vegetable stock*
*1 bay leaf*
*freshly ground black pepper*

■

Preparation time **10 minutes**
Cooking time **35 minutes**

**1** Cut the flesh of the pumpkin away from the skin, discard the seeds and chop the flesh roughly.
**2** Place the oil in a large saucepan and add the onion. Cook gently for 2 minutes. Stir in the spices and chopped pumpkin and cook for a further 2 minutes.
**3** Add the stock and bay leaf. Bring to the boil, cover and simmer for 25 minutes.
**4** Discard the bay leaf. Blend in a liquidiser to a smooth purée. Reheat, seasoning with black pepper to taste. Serve with croûtons if you wish.

*Low in calories, pumpkin makes a good base for a light golden coloured soup.*

*Microwave note*
**Place the oil and onion in a large bowl and cook on maximum power for 2 minutes. Stir in the spices and pumpkin and cook for 2 minutes. Add the stock and cook for 10 minutes. Proceed as recipe.**

*Pumpkin soup*

| Pumpkin soup |
| --- |
| *Per portion:* |
| **Calories 60** |
| Fat 4g |
| Fibre 2g |

# ROSY BEET SOUP

## SERVES 4

*1 tablespoon sunflower oil*
*100 g/4 oz onion, chopped*
*100 g/4 oz potato, diced*
*1 celery stick, chopped*
*350 g/12 oz whole uncooked beetroot,*
*peeled and diced*
*225 g/8 oz tomatoes, peeled and*
*chopped, or 1 (225-g/8-oz) can*
*tomatoes*
*900 ml/1½ pints vegetable stock*
*2 tablespoons cider vinegar*
*2 bay leaves*
*freshly ground black pepper*
*4 tablespoons natural yogurt*

■

*Preparation time* **15 minutes**
*Cooking time* **1 hour 25 minutes**

**1** Heat the oil in a large saucepan and add the onion, potato and celery. Cook gently for 2 minutes. Add the beetroot and cook for a further 3 minutes.
**2** Stir in the tomatoes, stock, cider vinegar and bay leaves and bring to the boil. Reduce the heat and simmer for 1¼ hours or until the beetroot is quite soft.
**3** Discard the bay leaves. Blend the soup in a liquidiser to a smooth purée. Reheat gently, seasoning with black pepper to taste. Garnish each serving with a swirl of yogurt.

*Beetroot is a good source of B vitamins, many minerals and fibre and deserves to be made more of in the diet. This soup is ideal for chilly autumn days. It is important to add the vinegar; without the acid the beetroot will cook to a strange brown colour.*

| Rosy beet soup | |
|---|---|
| *Per portion:* | |
| Calories | 100 |
| Fat | 4g |
| Fibre | 4g |

*Rosy beet soup*

*Freezing and Microwave note*
**Freeze in a firm container after blending in a liquidiser. Defrost at room temperature or in the microwave on defrost setting for 15 minutes. Reheat on full power for 8 minutes or until hot. Season and garnish as recipe.**

**Leek gougère**

**Per portion:**

Calories 360

Fat 21g

Fibre 6g

**Cauliflower & pasta supreme**

**Per portion:**

Calories 330

Fat 12g

Fibre 10g

*Freezing note*

**Choux pastry freezes well but gougère itself is not an ideal dish for freezing. One alternative, using the same ingredients, would be to make individual choux puffs. Wrap the completely cooled choux puffs in polythene bags and freeze until required. They are best defrosted at room temperature, filled and then reheated in the oven for 10 minutes.**

# Leek Gougère

### SERVES 4

*Pastry*
150 ml/¼ pint cold water
50 g/2 oz soft vegetable margarine
65 g/2½ oz 85% plain wheatmeal flour, sifted
2 free-range eggs
50 g/2 oz Gruyère cheese, finely grated
pinch of mustard powder
**Filling**
575 g/1¼ lb leeks
20 g/¾ oz soft vegetable margarine
20 g/¾ oz 85% plain wheatmeal flour
250 ml/8 fl oz skimmed milk
freshly ground black pepper

■

Preparation time **30 minutes**
Cooking time **40 minutes**
Oven temperature **220 C, 425 F, gas 7**
**190 C, 375 F, gas 5**

■

**1** Lightly oil a gratin dish or similar shallow oval, ovenproof dish.
**2** Place the water and margarine in a pan and heat until the margarine has melted. Turn up the heat to let the mixture boil, then quickly add the flour. Beat in well and remove from the heat. Continue beating until the mixture is smooth and glossy and leaves the sides of the pan.
**3** Cool slightly. Add one egg and beat in thoroughly before adding the second. Beat well, add the Gruyère and mustard.
**4** Pipe or spoon rosettes of the mixture around the edge of the dish. Bake for 20 minutes. Reduce the oven temperature and continue to cook for a further 10 minutes.
**5** While the pastry is baking, prepare the filling. Trim away the roots and coarse leaves from the leeks. Cut into 1-cm/½-in slices and plunge into a small amount of boiling water. Cook for 6–8 minutes. Drain, reserving the cooking liquid.
**6** Melt the margarine and stir in the flour. Cook for 1 minute. Gradually add the milk and enough of the cooking liquid from the leeks to make a fairly thick sauce. Add the leeks and season with

pepper. Simmer until the pastry is ready, pour into the centre of the dish and serve.

*Adding cheese to choux pastry makes a tasty base for a creamy sauce.*

# Cauliflower and Pasta Supreme

### SERVES 4

100 g/4 oz wholemeal pasta shapes
2 leeks · 1 large cauliflower
25 g/1 oz soft vegetable margarine
100 g/4 oz button mushrooms
25 g/1 oz 85% plain wheatmeal flour
300 ml/½ pint skimmed milk
100 g/4 oz Cheddar cheese, grated
freshly ground black pepper
2 tablespoons sesame seeds

■

Preparation time **25 minutes**
Cooking time **35 minutes**

■

**1** Cook the pasta in boiling water for 10–12 minutes until just tender. Drain.
**2** Trim the leeks and cut into 1-cm/½-in slices. Cut the cauliflower into florets and place both in a small amount of boiling water in a large pan. Cook for about 8 minutes. Drain, reserving the cooking water. Transfer the vegetables to a flameproof casserole and keep warm.
**3** Melt the margarine in a pan, add the mushrooms and cook for 2–3 minutes, then stir in the flour. Stirring constantly, add the milk and enough of the cooking water from the vegetables to make a smooth sauce. Add two-thirds of the cheese and simmer. Season with pepper. Stir in the pasta and heat through.
**4** Light the grill and pour the sauce over the vegetables. Top with the remaining Cheddar and the sesame seeds and grill until a bubbling golden brown.

*Wholemeal pasta and extra vegetables add protein to the good old favourite, cauliflower cheese, and turn this into a perfectly balanced complete meal.*

### Microwave note

**At stage 3, melt the margarine in a large casserole dish on full power for 30 seconds. Stir in the flour and cook for 30 seconds. Add the milk and heat for 2 minutes. Gradually add the stock and beat well. Add the mushrooms and cheese and cook for 2 minutes. Add the pasta and heat through for 1 minute. Proceed as recipe.**

*Leek gougère;
Cauliflower and pasta
supreme*

*Microwave note*
**The leek filling can be prepared in the microwave. Place the butter or margarine in a casserole dish with the sliced leeks and cook on full power for 5 minutes. Heat the milk on full power for 2 minutes. Stir the flour into the leeks and gradually add the milk. Season and heat in the microwave on full power for a further 3 minutes.**

*Swede and leek roulade*

**Swede and leek roulade**

| Per portion: | |
|---|---|
| Calories 180 | |
| Fat 10g | |
| Fibre 4g | |

# SWEDE AND LEEK ROULADE

## SERVES 4

*225 g/8 oz swede, peeled and diced*
*2 tablespoons skimmed milk*
*freshly ground black pepper*
*3 large free-range eggs*
### *Filling*
*225 g/8 oz leeks*
*25 g/1 oz unsalted butter or soft vegetable margarine*
*25 g/1 oz plain wholemeal flour*
*200 ml/7 fl oz skimmed milk*
*freshly ground black pepper*
*curly endive to garnish*
*(optional)*

■

*Preparation time* **25 minutes**
*Cooking time* **1 hour 10 minutes**
*Oven temperature* **200 C, 400 F, gas 6**

■

**1** Line and grease a 23 x 33-cm/9 x 13-in Swiss roll tin.
**2** Place the swede in a pan of cold water and bring to the boil, reduce the heat and simmer for 30–35 minutes or until really soft. Drain and mash with the milk and pepper to taste.
**3** Prepare the filling. Trim the leeks and slice finely. Melt the butter or margarine over a low heat and add the leeks. Cover and cook gently for 10 minutes until the leeks are just soft.
**4** Stir in the flour thoroughly and gradually add the milk, stirring well to form a smooth sauce. Season and set aside.
**5** Separate the eggs. Beat the egg yolks into the mashed swede. Whisk the egg whites until they form stiff peaks and gently fold into the swede mixture with a metal spoon. Pour into the prepared tin and smooth the top. Bake for 15–20 minutes until just firm to the touch.
**6** While the roulade is in the oven, reheat the leek sauce. Place a sheet of greaseproof paper on the worktop and as soon as the roulade is ready, invert on top of the paper and lift tin. Carefully peel off the paper – if it sticks place a damp cloth on top of the paper for a few seconds before trying again. Spread the leek sauce on top and quickly roll up like a Swiss roll, using the greaseproof paper as a guide. Slice and serve at once, garnished with curly endive, if preferred.

*An attractive and light dish which transforms swede into something special.*

*Hazelnut-stuffed courgettes*

# HAZELNUT-STUFFED MARROW

## SERVES 4

*1 medium marrow, or 675g/1½lb courgettes*
*100g/4oz wholemeal breadcrumbs*
*50g/2oz hazelnuts, ground*
*50g/2oz walnuts, ground*
*50g/2oz onion, chopped*
*1 tablespoon oil*
*100g/4oz button mushrooms, chopped*
*½ teaspoon chopped fresh sage*
*1 tablespoon chopped parsley*
*1 tablespoon tomato purée*
*1 free-range egg*
*freshly ground black pepper*
*50g/2oz farmhouse Cheddar cheese, finely grated*
*2 teaspoons sesame seeds*

■

*Preparation time* **25 minutes**
*Cooking time* **35 minutes**
*Oven temperature* **200C, 400F, gas 6**

■

**1** Cut the marrow into four 2.5-cm/1-in slices, or trim and halve the courgettes.

Scoop out the seeds and plunge the rings or courgette halves into a pan of boiling water. Cook for 2 minutes; alternatively, steam for 5 minutes. Drain and set aside while preparing the filling.
**2** Place the breadcrumbs, hazelnuts and walnuts in a mixing bowl. Cook the onion in the oil for 2 minutes without browning. Add the mushrooms to the pan. Heat through, then add to the mixing bowl.
**3** Place the sage and parsley in the bowl and beat in the tomato purée and egg. Season with pepper.
**4** Place the marrow rings or courgette halves in an ovenproof dish. Arrange the stuffing in the centre of each ring or half, pressing down firmly. Scatter the grated cheese and sesame seeds on top. Place 2 tablespoons cold water in the dish, cover with foil and bake for 30 minutes. Remove foil and bake uncovered for the final 5 minutes to brown. Serve at once.

*Marrow is remarkably low in calories but tends to have rather a bland taste. This makes it the perfect vehicle for stuffing – as in these tasty and nutritious marrow rings. The alternative of courgettes, shown in our picture, is equally good.*

**Hazelnut-stuffed marrow**

| *Per portion:* |
| --- |
| **Calories 340** |
| **Fat 22g** |
| **Fibre 9g** |

| Cannellini goulash | |
| --- | --- |
| **Per portion:** | |
| Calories 210 | |
| Fat 4g | |
| Fibre 16g | |

| Chick-peas with tomatoes | |
| --- | --- |
| **Per portion:** | |
| Calories 140 | |
| Fat 0g | |
| Fibre 11g | |

# CANNELLINI GOULASH

## SERVES 4

100g/4oz onion, chopped
1 celery stick, chopped
175g/6oz carrots, scrubbed and diced
100g/4oz potato, scrubbed and diced
1 tablespoon sunflower oil
175g/6oz cannellini beans, soaked overnight
1 (425-g/15-oz) can tomatoes
600ml/1 pint vegetable stock
1 red pepper, deseeded and chopped
1 tablespoon paprika
2 bay leaves
freshly ground black pepper
2 tablespoons natural yogurt

■

Preparation time **10 minutes, plus overnight soaking**
Cooking time **1 hour 35 minutes**
Oven temperature **190C, 375F, gas 5**

■

**1** Cook the onion, celery, carrot and potato gently in the oil for 2 minutes. Add the drained beans, tomatoes, stock, pepper, paprika and bay leaves. Bring to the boil, transfer to an ovenproof dish and bake for 1½ hours or until the beans are tender. Season to taste and stir in the yogurt.

Cannellini beans, or white kidney beans as they are sometimes called, make a lovely addition to this rich and nutritious vegetable goulash. Serve with wholemeal pasta for a perfectly balanced intake of protein.

# CHICK-PEAS WITH TOMATOES

## SERVES 4

1 tablespoon olive oil
100g/4oz onion, chopped
2 cloves garlic, crushed
225g/8oz potatoes, scrubbed and diced
¼ teaspoon ground cumin
1 red pepper, deseeded and chopped
175g/6oz courgettes, sliced
1 (425-g/15-oz) can tomatoes, chopped
1 (425-g/15-oz) can chick-peas, drained
1 tablespoon tomato purée
¼ teaspoon yeast extract
2 tablespoons cold water
freshly ground black pepper
1 tablespoon chopped parsley

■

Preparation time **15 minutes**
Cooking time **30 minutes**

■

**1** Heat the oil in a large saucepan and add the onion, garlic and potato and cook gently for 2 minutes. Stir in the cumin and cook for a further minute.
**2** Stir in the pepper, courgettes, tomatoes, chick-peas, tomato purée, yeast extract and the cold water. Bring to the boil, cover and simmer for 20–25 minutes until the potatoes are tender.
**3** Season to taste with black pepper and stir in the parsley.

Chick-peas, like all pulses, are a good source of protein and fibre. Using canned chick-peas saves time in making this quick supper dish. Serve with couscous or with brown rice or wholemeal pasta.

**Note**

If serving with couscous, allow 225 g/ 8 oz for four servings. Traditionally, couscous is cooked in a specially designed couscousier, being steamed gently in the vapours from the sauce as it cooks below. If you do not have a couscousier, an equally tasty way of cooking couscous is to 'roast' it in a heavy-based frying pan without any fat for 2 minutes, then gradually add hot vegetable stock a little at a time, stirring constantly so the grains swell and absorb the stock. Continue in this way until the couscous is soft. Serve at once with the chick-pea and tomato sauce.

*Cannellini goulash;
Chick-peas with tomatoes*

**Brazil bake**

*Per portion:*

Calories 380

Fat 27g

Fibre 8g

*Microwave note*

**Nut roasts such as this can be cooked in the microwave to save time but they lack the appetising colour of roasts cooked more slowly in the oven. The microwave is, however, invaluable in reheating slices of nut roast; allow 2 minutes on full power for each portion.**

# BRAZIL BAKE

### SERVES 6

*225 g/8 oz Brazil nuts*
*225 g/8 oz wholemeal breadcrumbs*
*225 g/8 oz carrots, scrubbed and grated*
*175 g/6 oz onion, chopped*
*3 celery sticks, sliced*
*1 red pepper, deseeded and chopped*
*1 teaspoon dried or 2 teaspoons fresh marjoram*
*freshly ground black pepper*
*3 free-range eggs*
*3 tablespoons tomato purée*

■

*Preparation time **25 minutes***
*Cooking time **45 minutes***
*Oven temperature **190 C, 375 F, gas 5***

**1** Line and lightly oil a 20-cm/8-in ring tin or a 450-g/1-lb loaf tin. If using the loaf tin, the above quantities should be halved.
**2** Grind the nuts or chop very finely. Mix with the breadcrumbs.
**3** Mix together the carrot, onion, celery and pepper.
**4** Add the marjoram and season with pepper. Beat in the eggs and tomato purée, adding a little water to mix.
**5** Pile into the prepared ring mould or loaf tin and smooth down the top. Bake for 45 minutes. Serve hot or cold. Chopped fresh vegetables make a crunchy addition.

*The combination of nuts and grains (wholemeal breadcrumbs) makes a well balanced protein dish.*

*Brazil bake; Tortilla*

# TORTILLA

### SERVES 4

*225 g / 8 oz potatoes*
*1½ tablespoons olive oil*
*4 free-range eggs*
*freshly ground black pepper*
*1 tablespoon chopped parsley to*
*garnish*

■

Preparation time **30 minutes**
Cooking time **25 minutes**

■

**1** Scrub the potatoes and cut into 5-cm/2-in pieces. Place in a pan of cold water and bring to the boil. Reduce heat and simmer for 15 minutes until tender. Drain and leave to cool before dicing.

**2** Place the oil in a 15-cm/6-in omelette pan and heat. Add the potatoes and cook for 3–4 minutes to heat through.

**3** Beat the eggs together in a jug and pour into the pan. Stir around to help them set evenly, but stop stirring when they are firming up. Run a palette knife around the edges to neaten and continue cooking to set the eggs. Flip the tortilla over to finish cooking and invert on to a plate. Season with pepper and garnish with parsley.

*This traditional Spanish dish can be served hot, or can be left to cool and served with a side salad. If liked, add two fresh, peeled and chopped tomatoes to the potatoes in the pan for a more colourful dish.*

| Tortilla | |
|---|---|
| *Per portion:* | |
| Calories 190 | |
| Fat 12g | |
| Fibre 1g | |

Baked red cabbage;
Parsnip and potato
cakes

# BAKED RED CABBAGE

### SERVES 4

*350 g/12 oz red cabbage, shredded
½ celery stick, chopped
50 g/2 oz onion, sliced
1 small dessert apple, cored and diced
25 g/1 oz raisins
250 ml/8 fl oz cold water
1 tablespoon cider vinegar
⅛ teaspoon ground cinnamon
⅛ teaspoon ground coriander*

■

*Preparation time* **10 minutes**
*Cooking time* **45 minutes**
*Oven temperature* **180 C, 350 F, gas 4**

■

**1** Place one half of the cabbage in an ovenproof casserole dish and add the celery, onion, apple and raisins. Cover with the remaining cabbage. Mix together the water, vinegar and spices and pour on to the cabbage. Cover tightly and bake for 45 minutes. Serve at once.

*Red cabbage makes a colourful accompaniment to many main courses. Although it is not such a good source of carotene – the plant form of vitamin A – as dark green cabbage, it contains many other valuable vitamins, minerals and fibre.*

# PARSNIP AND POTATO CAKES

### SERVES 4

*225 g/8 oz potatoes
225 g/8 oz parsnips
50 g/2 oz onion, chopped
15 g/½ oz butter or soft vegetable margarine
freshly ground black pepper
1 free-range egg
1 tablespoon sesame seeds
2 tablespoons wholemeal breadcrumbs
1–2 tablespoons oil*

**Garnish**
*tomato wedges
parsley sprigs*

■

*Preparation time* **25 minutes, plus 15 minutes to chill**
*Cooking time* **30 minutes**

■

**1** Peel the potatoes and parsnips and cut into 5-cm/2-in pieces. Place in a pan of cold water and bring to the boil. Reduce the heat and simmer for 15–20 minutes until soft. Drain.
**2** While the vegetables are cooking, fry the onion lightly in the butter or margarine for 2 minutes. When the vegetables are cooked and drained, mash with the onion mixture. Do not make the mixture too soft or it will not hold its shape. Season with pepper and leave to cool.
**3** Divide the mixture into four. Form each quarter into a burger shape. Beat the egg and pour into a shallow dish. In a second dish mix the sesame seeds and breadcrumbs together. Coat each burger first in the egg, then in the crumb mixture and shake off any excess. Place on a plate and chill in the refrigerator for 15 minutes.
**4** Heat the oil in a frying pan and add the parsnip and potato cakes. Cook for 4 minutes on each side, until a deep golden colour. Remove and serve at once. Garnish with tomato wedges and parsley sprigs.

*Shallow fry these parsnip and potato cakes in a very small amount of oil and heat up the oil before adding the cakes to the pan to quickly seal the outside of the food. This cuts down the amount of oil absorbed, keeping down the calorie and fat intake.*

**Baked red cabbage**
*Per portion:*
Calories 50
Fat 0g
Fibre 4g

*Freezing and Microwave note*
**Freeze after cooking by arranging each cake on a piece of foil and covering well. Defrost in the microwave on defrost setting for 4 minutes. Then heat through at full power for 3 minutes.**

**Parsnip and potato cakes**
*Per portion:*
Calories 200
Fat 11g
Fibre 4g

**Waldorf salad**

*Per portion:*

Calories 160

Fat 9g

Fibre 3g

*Waldorf salad; Cabbage and sesame stir-fry (below)*

**Cabbage and sesame stir-fry**

*Per portion:*

Calories 110

Fat 7g

Fibre 4g

# CABBAGE AND SESAME STIR-FRY

### SERVES 4

*100g/4oz onion, chopped*
*450g/1lb white cabbage, shredded*
*1 tablespoon sesame oil*
*2 tablespoons sesame seeds*
*freshly ground black pepper*

■

*Preparation time **10 minutes***
*Cooking time **6 minutes***

■

**1** Cook the onion and cabbage in the sesame oil in a saucepan over a low heat for 5 minutes, until the cabbage has lost its bite. Stir in the sesame seeds and cook for a further minute before seasoning.

*A tasty accompaniment to many dishes.*

# WALDORF SALAD

### SERVES 4

*4 celery sticks, chopped*
*50 g/2 oz walnuts, chopped*
*50 g/2 oz raisins*
*2 crisp dessert apples, cored and diced*
*1 tablespoon mayonnaise*
*1 tablespoon natural yogurt*
*freshly ground black pepper*

■

*Preparation time **20 minutes***

■

**1** Mix together the celery, walnuts, raisins and apples.
**2** In a serving bowl, toss in the mayonnaise and yogurt and lightly season with pepper. Serve at once.

*This crunchy classic salad makes a good side dish or, served on a bed of shredded lettuce, a light starter, full of fibre and low in calories.*

# BAKED APPLES

### SERVES 4

*4 medium cooking apples (Bramleys are best)*
*75 g/3 oz ground almonds*
*25 g/1 oz wholemeal breadcrumbs*
*grated rind of $\frac{1}{2}$ lemon*
*1 tablespoon orange juice*
*1 tablespoon clear honey*
*2 tablespoons cold water*

■

*Preparation time **10 minutes***
*Cooking time **35–50 minutes***
*Oven temperature **180 C, 350 F, gas 4***

■

**1** Wipe the apples. Remove the core and make a slit around the middle of each apple.
**2** Mix together the almonds, breadcrumbs, lemon rind, orange juice and honey, and use to fill the apple centres. Place the apples in a shallow ovenproof dish and place the cold water in the base of the dish. Bake for 35–50 minutes, depending on the size of the apples, until soft. Serve at once with yogurt.

*An old family favourite, baked apples make a cheap dessert at this time of the year, using the best, unblemished apples from the new season's harvest. The tasty almond stuffing makes a pleasant change from the usual fruity filling.*

| Baked apples | |
|---|---|
| ***Per portion:*** | |
| **Calories** | 120 |
| **Fat** | 10g |
| **Fibre** | 4g |

*Microwave note*
**Bake the apples in the microwave on full power for 6–7 minutes; the exact time varies with size and variety of apple.**

*Baked apples*

# WINTER

## DECEMBER · JANUARY · FEBRUARY

It may be cold outside but there is a huge array of fresh fruits and vegetables in store to liven up wintry days. Cabbages are plentiful – there are red, white and green to choose from. Brussels sprouts are also good value, as are broccoli and cauliflowers. Carrots, swedes, turnips, parsnips and leeks are cheap and plentiful and imported supplies of celery, sweet potatoes and fennel are available too.

Oranges, grapefruits, lemons and other imported fruits, including the more exotic figs and dates, boost home-grown apples and pears.

### WINTER MENUS

#### 1

*Winter salad bowl with hot garlic bread*

*Almond roast with savoury baked potatoes and broccoli or Brussels sprouts*

*Fruit compote with Greek-style strained yogurt*

#### 2

*Walnut-stuffed mushrooms*

*Winter bean pot with baked potato and lightly cooked cabbage*

*Fresh fruit salad and yogurt*

#### 3

*Brussels soup*

*Oaty-topped root pie*

*Apple and orange charlotte*

# MINESTRONE SOUP

### SERVES 4

2 tablespoons olive oil
100g/4oz onion, chopped
2 cloves garlic, crushed
225g/8oz carrot, scrubbed and diced
225g/8oz parsnip or swede, peeled and
diced
100g/4oz potato, diced
100g/4oz pinto beans, soaked
overnight
1 (425-g/15-oz) can tomatoes
1 tablespoon tomato purée
½ teaspoon marjoram or oregano
2 bay leaves
750ml/1¼ pints vegetable stock
50g/2oz white cabbage
50g/2oz wholemeal pasta shapes
freshly ground black pepper
**Garnish**
grated Parmesan cheese
finely chopped parsley

■

Preparation time **20 minutes, plus
overnight soaking**
Cooking time **1 hour 35 minutes**

■

**1** Heat the oil in a large saucepan and stir in the onion, garlic and carrot. Cook gently for 2 minutes. Stir in the parsnip or swede and the potato and cook for a further minute.
**2** Add the drained pinto beans, tomatoes, tomato purée, marjoram or oregano, bay leaves and stock and bring to the boil. Cover and simmer for 1¼ hours.
**3** Shred the white cabbage finely and stir into the soup with the wholemeal pasta. Cook for 15 minutes or until the pasta is tender. Season with black pepper to taste and serve, garnished with Parmesan and parsley.

Adding some wholemeal pasta to the soup just before serving balances the protein in the beans.

# BRUSSELS SOUP

### SERVES 4

225g/8oz leeks
1 tablespoon sunflower oil
1 celery stick, chopped
225g/8oz Brussels sprouts, trimmed
and chopped
½ teaspoon dried thyme
1 bay leaf
1 litre/1¾ pints vegetable stock
100g/4oz green split peas, soaked
overnight
150ml/¼ pint skimmed milk
freshly ground black pepper

Microwave note
**Place the oil, leeks and
celery in a large
casserole dish, cover
and cook on maximum
power for 2 minutes.
Stir in the sprouts and
continue to cook for 2
further minutes. Add
the split peas, stock
and herbs and cook for
20 minutes, stirring
after 10 minutes.
Proceed with stage 4.**

*Preparation time* **10 minutes, plus
overnight soaking**
*Cooking time* **45 minutes**

■

**1** Trim the roots and coarse top leaves
from the leeks. Shred, and wash
thoroughly.
**2** Heat the oil and stir in the leeks and
celery. Cook gently for 2 minutes,
covered. Stir in the sprouts and cook for a
further minute.
**3** Add the thyme, bay leaf and vegetable
stock plus the drained split peas. Bring to
the boil, cover and simmer for 40 minutes
or until the split peas are quite soft.
**4** Discard the bay leaf. Blend in a

liquidiser to a smooth purée and reheat,
stirring in the skimmed milk and seasoning to taste with black pepper.
Wholemeal croûtons give texture, if
preferred.

*The addition of Brussels sprouts to this
winter soup gives a rich colour and
flavour. Split peas, like lentils, can be
cooked successfully in the microwave to
save time; larger pulses cook less well.*

Minestrone soup;
Brussels soup

| Brussels soup | |
|---|---|
| **Per portion:** | |
| Calories 150 | |
| Fat 4g | |
| Fibre 8g | |

| Walnut-stuffed mushrooms | |
|---|---|
| *Per portion:* | |
| Calories 250 | |
| Fat 20g | |
| Fibre 3g | |

*Cheesy baked eggs*

| Cheesy baked eggs | |
|---|---|
| *Per portion:* | |
| Calories 140 | |
| Fat 10g | |
| Fibre 0g | |

*Microwave note*

**This recipe can be prepared in the microwave. The yolk of the egg must be pierced before sprinkling the cheese on top. Cook on half power for 1½–1¾ minutes.**

# CHEESY BAKED EGGS

### SERVES 4

*4 large free-range eggs*
*50 g/2 oz cheese, grated*
*freshly ground black pepper*
*I tablespoon chopped parsley to garnish*

■

*Preparation time **5 minutes***
*Cooking time **7 minutes***
*Oven temperature **180 C, 350 F, gas 4***

■

**I** Lightly butter four ramekin dishes. Break the eggs into the dishes. Sprinkle the cheese on top of the eggs, with pepper to season.
**2** Place the ramekins in a dish half-filled with water and bake for 6–7 minutes or until the whites of the eggs are just firm. Garnish with parsley and serve at once with wholemeal bread.

*Cheddar cheese works well in this recipe, but a small amount of crumbled Stilton gives a lovely rich flavour.*

# WALNUT-STUFFED MUSHROOMS

### SERVES 4

*I tablespoon olive oil*
*8 large open mushrooms*
*50 g/2 oz onion, chopped*
*I clove garlic, crushed*
*75 g/3 oz walnuts, ground or chopped*
*50 g/2 oz wholemeal breadcrumbs*
*I teaspoon chopped fresh or ½ teaspoon rubbed sage*
*I free-range egg*
*I tablespoon tomato purée*
*freshly ground black pepper*
*50 g/2 oz double Gloucester cheese, grated*
*chopped parsley to garnish*

■

*Preparation time **15 minutes***
*Cooking time **25 minutes***
*Oven temperature **200 C, 400 F, gas 6***

■

**I** Lightly oil a shallow ovenproof dish.
**2** Wipe the mushrooms and remove the stalks. Place the mushrooms in the dish.
**3** Cook the onion and garlic lightly in the oil for 2 minutes.
**4** Mix the walnuts with the onion and garlic, breadcrumbs and sage. Bind with the egg and tomato purée and season with pepper. Stuff the mixture into the mushrooms and press into the base. Sprinkle the cheese on top. Bake for 20 minutes. Garnish with parsley and serve hot.

*A fibre-rich and attractive first course.*

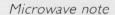

# ALMOND ROAST

## SERVES 6

225 g / 8 oz button mushrooms
175 g / 6 oz carrot, scrubbed and grated
1 onion, chopped
1 celery stick, diced
225 g / 8 oz ground almonds
225 g / 8 oz wholemeal breadcrumbs
1 tablespoon finely grated lemon rind
1 teaspoon chopped fresh or ½ teaspoon
dried thyme
1 tablespoon chopped parsley
3 free-range eggs
freshly ground black pepper

■

Preparation time **20 minutes**
Cooking time **45 minutes**
Oven temperature **190 C, 375 F, gas 5**

**1** Line and lightly oil a 20-cm/8-in ring tin or 450-g / 1-lb loaf tin. If using the loaf tin, the quantities should be halved.
**2** Wipe the mushrooms and chop very finely. Place all the vegetables in a mixing bowl.
**3** Stir in the almonds, breadcrumbs, lemon rind, thyme and parsley. Mix in thoroughly.
**4** Beat the eggs together and mix into the dry ingredients, adding a little water to bind the mixture together. Season with pepper and place in the prepared tin. Smooth the top, cover with foil and bake for 35 minutes. Remove the foil and continue cooking for a further 10 minutes. Serve hot or leave to cool thoroughly before serving sliced, cold. A festive presentation is shown below.

*If using the ring tin, serve lightly boiled Brussels sprouts in the centre.*

*Microwave note*
**Cook the Walnut-stuffed mushrooms in the microwave on full power for 4 minutes, then finish off under a hot grill to just brown the top.**

*Almond roast; Walnut-stuffed mushrooms*

| Almond roast | |
| --- | --- |
| *Per portion:* | |
| Calories 350 | |
| Fat 25g | |
| Fibre 10g | |

## Potato layer bake

**Per portion:**

| | |
|---|---|
| Calories | 220 |
| Fat | 6g |
| Fibre | 4g |

Winter bean pot;
Potato layer bake

# POTATO LAYER BAKE

### SERVES 4

100g/4oz onion, sliced
675g/1½ lb potatoes, peeled and sliced
1 clove garlic, crushed (optional)
freshly ground black pepper
75g/3oz farmhouse Cheddar cheese,
finely grated
skimmed milk
chopped parsley to garnish

Preparation time **10 minutes**
Cooking time **1¼–1½ hours**
Oven temperature **180C, 350F, gas 4**

■

**1** Lightly oil a shallow ovenproof dish.
**2** Arrange the onion and potato slices in layers with the garlic, if using. Season with pepper and scatter the Cheddar on top. Pour over sufficient skimmed milk to come almost to the top of the potatoes, and bake for 1¼–1½ hours until tender. Garnish with freshly chopped parsley.

*This method of cooking potatoes makes a superb side dish for more formal meals. If preferred, a little crushed garlic can be added to give extra flavour.*

# WINTER BEAN POT

## SERVES 4

2 leeks, trimmed and washed
1 tablespoon sunflower oil
100 g/4 oz onion, chopped
2 cloves garlic, crushed
225 g/8 oz carrots, scrubbed and diced
225 g/8 oz parsnip, peeled and diced
100 g/4 oz turnip, peeled and diced
1 (425-g/15-oz) can tomatoes
1 tablespoon tomato purée
1.25 litres/2¼ pints vegetable stock
1 bay leaf
½ teaspoon dried basil or oregano
2 tablespoons pot barley
100 g/4 oz butter beans, soaked overnight
75 g/3 oz pinto beans, soaked overnight
freshly ground black pepper

■

Preparation time **10 minutes, plus overnight soaking**
Cooking time **1 hour 20 minutes**
Oven temperature **190 C, 375 F, gas 5**

■

**1** Slice the leeks into 1-cm/½ in rings.
**2** Heat the oil in a large saucepan or in the base of a flameproof casserole. Cook the onion, garlic and leek for 2 minutes. Then stir in the carrot, parsnip and turnip and cook for 1 minute.
**3** Add the tomatoes and tomato purée and stir in thoroughly. Add the stock, bay leaf, basil or oregano, pot barley and drained beans. Mix in well, bring to the boil, then bake for 1–1¼ hours or until the beans are tender. Season and serve.

*Warming dishes like this one are perfect for cold winter evenings. The combination of beans, pot barley and root vegetables is irresistible. Serve with jacket potatoes topped with grated cheese to increase the protein in this meal.*

| Winter bean pot | |
|---|---|
| **Per portion:** | |
| Calories 240 | |
| Fat 4g | |
| Fibre 15g | |

*Aduki and pepper quiche; Oaty-topped root pie*

**Aduki and pepper quiche**

*Per portion:*

Calories 330

Fat 19g

Fibre 6g

*Microwave note*

**The flan case can be baked blind in the microwave for 4 minutes on full power if preferred. Proceed as recipe. The quiche can also be reheated in the microwave on medium power for 5 minutes.**

# ADUKI AND PEPPER QUICHE

### SERVES 4

**Pastry**
*100g/4oz plain wholemeal flour
50g/2oz soft vegetable margarine
cold water to mix*
**Filling**
*50g/2oz aduki beans, soaked overnight
1 small onion, chopped
1 tablespoon oil
50g/2oz button mushrooms
½ green pepper, chopped
2 free-range eggs
150ml/¼ pint natural yogurt
freshly ground black pepper
25g/1oz Cheddar cheese, grated
curly endive to garnish*

■

*Preparation time **20 minutes, plus overnight soaking and 15 minutes to chill***
*Cooking time **45 minutes***
*Oven temperature **200C, 400F, gas 6***

**1** Cook the aduki beans for 45–50 minutes, or 12 minutes at 6.75kg/15lb pressure in a pressure cooker and drain.
**2** Sift the flour into a mixing bowl and add the bran from the sieve. Rub in the margarine until the mixture resembles fine breadcrumbs. Place the bowl in the refrigerator to rest for 15 minutes.
**3** Cook the onion gently for 2 minutes in the oil. Stir in the mushrooms and pepper and cook for a further minute. Mix in the aduki beans and remove from the heat.
**4** Add enough cold water to the flour and margarine mixture to mix to a soft dough. Roll out on a lightly floured work surface, then use to line an 18-cm/7-in flan ring or dish. Bake blind for 10 minutes.
**5** Place the bean mixture in the flan case. In a bowl, beat together the eggs, yogurt and black pepper. Pour the mixture over the filling. Sprinkle the cheese on top. Return to the oven for 25–30 minutes until the filling is set. Serve hot or cold, garnished with curly endive.

*This substantial quiche is equally good served hot or cold. The beans add extra protein and fibre. Serve with a salad and wholemeal bread or a baked potato.*

# Oaty-Topped Root Pie

**SERVES 6**

***Pastry***

*175 g | 6 oz plain wholemeal flour*
*50 g | 2 oz rolled oats*
*100 g | 4 oz soft vegetable margarine*
*cold water to mix*
*skimmed milk to glaze*

***Filling***

*2 leeks, trimmed, washed and chopped*
*2 celery sticks, chopped*
*275 g | 10 oz carrots, scrubbed and diced*
*275 g | 10 oz parsnips, peeled and diced*
*40 g | 1½ oz soft vegetable margarine*
*3 tablespoons plain wholemeal flour*
*450 ml | ¾ pint vegetable stock*

■

*Preparation time* ***35 minutes, plus time to chill***
*Cooking time* ***35 minutes***
*Oven temperature* ***200 C, 400 F, gas 6***

■

**1** Place the flour and oats in a mixing bowl, reserving 1 tablespoon oats, and rub in the margarine, until the mixture resembles fine breadcrumbs. Place in the refrigerator to rest while preparing the filling.
**2** Melt the margarine in a pan and add the vegetables. Cook gently for 3 minutes. Stir in the flour and cook for 2 minutes. Gradually add the stock, stirring well to make a smooth sauce. Simmer for 10 minutes, stirring occasionally to prevent sticking. Remove from the heat and pour into a deep 900-ml / 1½-pint pie dish.
**3** Add just enough water to the pastry mixture to make a soft dough. Roll out on a lightly floured surface to a size slightly larger than the top of the pie dish. Cut a narrow strip of pastry from the edge and use to line the dampened rim of the pie dish. Brush with water, then top with the pastry lid. Trim edges, flute and glaze with milk. Sprinkle over the reserved oats. Bake for 30 minutes.

*Oats are a good source of a particular type of fibre which is known to help lower the level of cholesterol in the blood. One good way to increase the quantity of oats in the diet is to substitute oats for 25 g | 1 oz wholemeal flour in a basic pastry mixture using 100 g | 4 oz flour.*

**Oaty-topped root pie**
***Per portion:***
**Calories 360**
**Fat 20g**
**Fibre 8g**

*Microwave note*
**At stage 2, place the margarine and vegetables in a covered dish and cook on maximum power for 5 minutes. Add the flour and stock and return to cook for a further 5 minutes. Place in the pie dish and proceed with stage 3.**

**Lentil and potato pie**

*Per portion:*

Calories 300

Fat 6g

Fibre 10g

# LENTIL AND POTATO PIE

## SERVES 4

1 tablespoon olive oil
100 g/4 oz onion, chopped
1 celery stick, chopped
2 cloves garlic, crushed
100 g/4 oz open mushrooms, chopped
1 (425-g/15-oz) can tomatoes
1 green or red pepper, deseeded and chopped
1 tablespoon tomato purée
175 g/6 oz brown lentils
150 ml/$\frac{1}{4}$ pint vegetable stock
1 bay leaf
**Topping**
450 g/1 lb potatoes
knob of unsalted butter
dash of skimmed milk

■

Preparation time **10 minutes**
Cooking time **1 hour 25 minutes**

■

**1** Heat the oil and add the onion, celery and garlic. Cook gently for 2 minutes. Add the mushrooms, tomatoes, pepper, tomato purée, lentils, stock and bay leaf. Bring to the boil, cover and simmer for 1 hour until the lentils are quite soft.

**2** Meanwhile, peel the potatoes and cut into 5-cm/2-in pieces and place in cold water. Bring to the boil, reduce the heat and simmer steadily for 15–20 minutes until soft. Drain and mash with butter and a dash of skimmed milk to a smooth consistency.

**3** Heat the grill and warm a flameproof dish. Place the lentil mixture in the dish and top with the mashed potato. Grill for 5 minutes or until the top is crusty and brown. Serve with Brussels sprouts or a dark green leafy cabbage.

*Brown lentils are a good source of protein, fibre, minerals and B vitamins and are much lower in fat than the conventional minced meat used in shepherd's pie. But they are surprisingly tasty too and non-vegetarians will be won over by this simple supper dish.*

# BAKED RICE

## SERVES 4

225 g/8 oz long-grain brown rice
750 ml/1$\frac{1}{4}$ pints water
1 tablespoon tomato purée
$\frac{1}{2}$ teaspoon yeast extract
1 bay leaf
150 g/5 oz red lentils
175 g/6 oz carrots, scrubbed and sliced
175 g/6 oz sweet potato, scrubbed and diced
100 g/4 oz swede or parsnip, peeled and diced
100 g/4 oz onion, chopped
1 teaspoon cumin seeds
pinch of cayenne
$\frac{1}{2}$ teaspoon turmeric

*Preparation time **10 minutes***
*Cooking time **1 hour 10 minutes***
*Oven temperature **200 C, 400 F, gas 6***
***180 C, 350 F, gas 4***
■

**1** Place the rice in a large casserole dish with the water, tomato purée, yeast extract and bay leaf. Bake for 30 minutes.
**2** Turn down the oven temperature. Stir in the lentils, prepared vegetables, cumin seeds, cayenne and turmeric. Bake for a further 40 minutes.
**3** Transfer the baked rice to a serving dish and serve at once. Brussels sprouts make a good accompaniment.

*An unusual method of cooking rice in the oven with red lentils and nutritious root vegetables, including the flavourful sweet potato, now widely available at this time of year. Despite the name, sweet potatoes are not related to potatoes. Although first imported into Europe in the sixteenth century, this vegetable is not currently a popular ingredient in the English diet. But do experiment with it in this tasty dish.*

| Baked rice | |
|---|---|
| *Per portion:* | |
| Calories | 400 |
| Fat | 1g |
| Fibre | 11g |

*Baked rice; Lentil and potato pie*

## Microwave note

**Baked potatoes cook quickly in the microwave but lack the crisp skin obtained by cooking in the conventional oven. This recipe, however, works really well in the microwave. Wrap the scrubbed and pierced potatoes separately in pieces of kitchen paper and place on full power in the microwave. Cook for 20 minutes. Unwrap and leave to stand for 5 minutes before proceeding as recipe. Return the filled potatoes to the microwave for 3 minutes until the cheese has melted.**

### Cheesy baked potatoes

*Per portion:*

Calories 340

Fat 12g

Fibre 5g

### Chestnut pie

*Per portion:*

Calories 586

Fat 30g

Fibre 14g

# CHEESY BAKED POTATOES

### SERVES 4

4 (225-g/8-oz) potatoes
100g/4oz onion, chopped
1 tablespoon sunflower oil
100g/4oz mushrooms, diced
100g/4oz farmhouse Cheddar cheese, grated
a little skimmed milk
freshly ground black pepper

**Garnish**
halved tomato slices
parsley sprigs
curly endive

■

Preparation time **12 minutes**
Cooking time **1 hour 40 minutes**
Oven temperature **200C, 400F, gas 6**

■

**1** Scrub the potatoes and pierce the skins with a fork in six places. Bake for 1–1¼ hours until the insides are soft.
**2** Cook the onion in the oil gently for 3 minutes and stir in the mushrooms; cook for 1 minute, then set aside.
**3** When the potatoes are cooked, cut each one in half and scoop out the insides, retaining the skin. Mash the potato in a mixing bowl with the onion and mushroom mixture and half of the Cheddar, adding just enough milk to mix to a smooth texture. Season with pepper.
**4** Arrange the potato shells in a shallow ovenproof dish and pile in the potato mixture. Sprinkle the remaining cheese on top and return to the oven for 20 minutes until the cheese has melted and is bubbling. Serve garnished as shown.

*Baked potatoes make a good sustaining light meal when served with toppings such as cottage cheese, mushrooms and grated cheese, or make the perfect accompaniment to many main dishes when served with a little butter or margarine and lashings of black pepper. This recipe takes a little extra time to prepare, but the result is well worth the effort.*

# CHESTNUT PIE

### SERVES 6

**Filling**
225g/8oz chestnuts
2 celery sticks, chopped
175g/6oz onion, chopped
1 clove garlic, crushed
1 tablespoon sunflower oil
3 tablespoons chopped parsley
1 teaspoon dried or 2 teaspoons chopped fresh thyme
grated rind of ½ lemon
175g/6oz wholemeal breadcrumbs
2 free-range eggs
2–3 tablespoons vegetable stock
450g/1 lb Brussels sprouts
freshly ground black pepper
salad ingredients to garnish

**Pastry**
175g/6oz soft vegetable margarine
350g/12oz plain wholemeal flour
cold water to mix
beaten egg to glaze

■

Preparation time **50 minutes, plus 10 minutes to chill**
Cooking time **2 hours**
Oven temperature **200C, 400F, gas 6**
**180C, 350F, gas 4**

■

**1** Lightly oil a game pie mould, or oil a deep 15-cm/6-in round cake tin and line with greaseproof paper.
**2** Prepare the chestnuts by slitting the shells and skins with a knife, bringing them to the boil in water and simmering for 3 minutes. Peel away the chestnut skins. Chop the chestnuts finely.
**3** Cook the celery, onion and garlic together in the oil for a few minutes without browning. Stir into the chestnuts and add the parsley, thyme, lemon rind and breadcrumbs. Mix in thoroughly. Beat the eggs and add to the bowl with just enough stock to bind to a moist consistency. Garnish as shown.
**4** Make the pastry. Rub the margarine into the flour until the mixture resembles fine breadcrumbs. Chill for 10 minutes.
**5** Trim the sprouts and cook in boiling

Chestnut pie; Cheesy
baked potatoes

## Microwave note

**Slit the chestnut shells
and skins, rinse and
place the nuts in a
basin and cook on full
power for 5 minutes.
The skins will easily
peel away. Brussels
sprouts cook in around
8–10 minutes on full
power in the
microwave, if placed
with a little water in a
covered casserole dish.**

water for 15–20 minutes until really soft.
Drain and mash or chop finely and season.
**6** Add just enough cold water to the
pastry to make a soft dough. Roll out two-
thirds of the pastry to fit the base and
sides of the pie mould or tin and line.
Place one half of the chestnut mixture in
the base, top with sprouts, then place the
remaining chestnut mixture on top. Roll
out the remaining pastry and place on

top. Seal the edges and shape any pastry
trimmings into leaves to decorate. Glaze
with the beaten egg and bake for 20
minutes, then lower the oven temperature for a further 45 minutes. Leave in the
pie mould or tin to cool, or serve hot.

*A splendid winter pie which should be
made in a raised pie mould for best
results.*

**Creamy carrot and swede**

| Per portion: | |
|---|---|
| Calories | 70 |
| Fat | 2g |
| Fibre | 7g |

# CREAMY CARROT AND SWEDE

## SERVES 4

675 g| 1½ lb swede, scrubbed and diced
350 g| 12 oz carrots, scrubbed and diced
knob of unsalted butter
a little skimmed milk
freshly ground black pepper
parsley sprig to garnish

■

Preparation time **10 minutes**
Cooking time **50 minutes**

■

**1** Place the swede and carrots in a pan and just cover with cold water. Bring to the boil, then reduce the heat and simmer for 45 minutes until the vegetables are quite soft. Drain.
**2** Mash with butter and just enough skimmed milk to make a smooth purée. Season with pepper, reheat gently in a pan and serve at once, garnished with a sprig of parsley.

*Root vegetables are cheap and plentiful in winter months and this creamy purée transforms two favourite vegetables into something more sophisticated.*

# COLESLAW

## SERVES 4

2 red-skinned dessert apples, cored and diced
juice of ½ lemon
1 small white cabbage, shredded
225 g| 8 oz carrots, scrubbed and grated
2 celery sticks, sliced
1 small onion, grated or finely chopped
100 g| 4 oz raisins
2 tablespoons natural yogurt
2 tablespoons mayonnaise
1 tablespoon chopped parsley to garnish

■

Preparation time **15 minutes**

**Winter salad bowl**

| Per portion: | |
|---|---|
| Calories | 30 |
| Fat | 0g |
| Fibre | 4g |

**Coleslaw**

| Per portion: | |
|---|---|
| Calories | 220 |
| Fat | 8g |
| Fibre | 9g |

**1** Toss the apple in the lemon juice.
**2** Mix all the prepared vegetables together with the apple, raisins, yogurt and mayonnaise. Place in a serving dish and garnish with parsley. Serve.

*When the temperature drops we tend to neglect salads, but we should try to make room in our winter menus for raw vegetables with maximum vitamin C content. This classic coleslaw is easy to make, especially if you own a food processor.*

# WINTER SALAD BOWL

## SERVES 4

275 g| 10 oz red cabbage, shredded
3 celery sticks, chopped
1 large or 2 small oranges
bunch of watercress
1 tablespoon chopped parsley
freshly ground black pepper

■

Preparation time **15 minutes**

■

**1** Mix together the cabbage and celery.
**2** Stand the orange(s) on a chopping board and cut away the peel. Cut into slices, then cut each slice into small pieces and add to the bowl, with any juice that has run on to the board.
**3** Wash the watercress and trim any yellowing leaves and very coarse stalks. Add to the bowl with the chopped parsley and season lightly with pepper. Toss together thoroughly and serve.

*Red cabbage makes just as good an ingredient in a salad as white cabbage. This colourful recipe combines oranges and watercress too, the vitamin C in the orange enhancing the way in which the body absorbs the iron in the watercress. No dressing is needed as the juice from the oranges freshens the whole salad.*

*Creamy carrot and swede; Winter salad bowl; Coleslaw*

**Christmas pud**

**Per portion:**

Calories 520

Fat 15g

Fibre 15g

**Fruit compote**

**Per portion:**

Calories 140

Fat 0g

Fibre 5g (approx)

*Apple and orange charlotte*

## Microwave note

**Reheating Christmas pudding on Christmas Day can be done quickly in the microwave. Reheat for 4 minutes and leave to stand for 5 minutes before serving.**

## CHRISTMAS PUD

### SERVES 4

*175 g | 6 oz raisins
175 g | 6 oz sultanas
50 g | 2 oz dried apricots, chopped
1 banana, mashed
75 g | 3 oz Brazil nuts, chopped
100 g | 4 oz carrots, scrubbed and finely grated
grated rind and juice of ½ lemon
100 g | 4 oz wholemeal breadcrumbs
25 g | 1 oz plain wholemeal flour
2 teaspoons mixed spice
2 free-range eggs
150 ml | ¼ pint skimmed milk
1 tablespoon brandy, rum or orange juice*

■

*Preparation time **20 minutes**
Cooking time **6 hours, plus 2 hours reheating***

■

**1** Lightly grease a 1-kg/2-lb pudding basin. Have ready a double thickness layer of greaseproof paper to cover the top of the pudding and a pudding cloth, piece of foil or fitted lid to cover the basin.
**2** Place the prepared fruit, nuts, carrot and lemon rind and juice in a large mixing bowl. Stir in the breadcrumbs, flour and spice thoroughly. Beat together the eggs, milk and brandy, rum or orange juice and pour into the bowl, mixing in well.
**3** Place the mixture in a prepared basin and cover with greaseproof paper and either foil, cloth or lid. Steam for 6 hours, or cook in a pressure cooker by steaming for 30 minutes, then adding 6.75-kg/15-lb weights and cooking for a further 2 hours 45 minutes. Allow pressure to return to normal, slowly.
**4** To reheat the pudding on Christmas Day, steam for 2 hours, or pressure cook at 6.75-kg/15-lb pressure for 30 minutes.
**5** Serve with yogurt and decorate as shown.

*Makes one 1-kg/2-lb pudding. There is no need for the conventional sugar and suet in this tasty, fruity pudding recipe.*

## FRUIT COMPOTE

### SERVES 4

*225 g | 8 oz mixed dried fruit (prunes, apricots, pears, apple rings, figs)
600 ml | 1 pint cold water
juice of ½ lemon
juice of 1 orange
pinch of mixed spice*

■

*Preparation time **5 minutes, plus overnight standing***

■

**1** Place the dried fruit in a bowl. Heat the water with the lemon and orange juice and the spice. Pour over the fruit and leave to stand overnight. Reheat if liked.

*Dried fruits such as prunes, apricots and pears make a warming winter dessert which helps to supply fibre as well as valuable minerals. It is low in calories too.*

**Microwave note**

Place the dried fruit in a casserole. Pour over the water, lemon and orange juice and spice. Heat on full power for 8 minutes. Leave to stand for at least 1 hour before serving.

*Christmas pud; Fruit compote*

# APPLE AND ORANGE CHARLOTTE

## SERVES 4

*65 g/2½ oz soft vegetable margarine*
*50 g/2 oz desiccated coconut*
*100 g/4 oz wholemeal breadcrumbs*
*½ teaspoon ground cinnamon*
*25 g/1 oz demerara sugar*
*450 g/1 lb cooking apples*
*1 teaspoon lemon juice*
*1 large orange*
*1 tablespoon clear honey*
*1 tablespoon orange juice*

Preparation time **25 minutes**
Cooking time **30 minutes**
Oven temperature **190 C, 375 F, gas 5**

1 Melt the margarine over a low heat and stir in the coconut, breadcrumbs and cinnamon. Stirring constantly, heat through for 5 minutes until brown and crisp. Remove from the heat and stir in the sugar.

2 Peel and finely slice the cooking apples; cover the slices in cold water mixed with the lemon juice to prevent browning. Cut away the peel from the orange and slice horizontally, then cut each slice into four quarters. Drain the apple slices and arrange in an ovenproof soufflé dish with the chopped orange. Pour over the honey and orange juice and spread the coconut mixture on top. Bake for 20–25 minutes until the apple slices are just tender. Serve at once.

*A light, fruity dessert, best served hot with natural yogurt.*

| Apple and orange charlotte | |
|---|---|
| **Per portion:** | |
| Calories 360 | |
| Fat 21g | |
| Fibre 8g | |

**Microwave note**

Melt the margarine in the microwave and stir in the coconut, breadcrumbs and cinnamon. Cook on full power for 2 minutes. Stir well and cook for further 1 minute. Proceed as recipe.

# Index